THE WELL-SEASONED WOK

Martin Yan

Photography by Keith Ovregaard

MJF BOOKS

NEW YORK

Styling: **Susan Devaty**
Prop Styling: **Debbie Dicker**
Illustrations: **Pauline Phung**
Typography: **Classic Typography**
Book Production: **Schuettge & Carleton**

Props for Photography: Cottonwood, San Francisco (pgs. 88, 105, 177)
The Gardener, Berkeley, CA (pgs. 35, 80, 130, 136, 141, 153)
Linda Goldstone, San Francisco (pgs. 42, 77)
Phoenix Gallery, San Francisco (pg. 71)
Shiki, San Francisco (pgs. 98, 110, 144, 173)
Summer House, Mill Valley, CA (pgs. 64, 117, 159)

Back cover photo: Yin-Yang Chicken and Spinach Soup, recipe page 55

Published by MJF Books
Fine Communications
Two Lincoln Square
60 West 66th Street
New York, NY 10023

Library of Congress Catalog Card Number 97-75619
ISBN 1-56731-252-7
Printed in Singapore

This edition published by arrangement with Harlow & Ratner.

10 9 8 7 6 5 4 3 2 1

Acknowledgments

As the "Yan Can Cook" show approaches its 15th anniversary, it gives me great cause for joyous celebration. The loyal support of fans and friends has made the previous cookbooks bestsellers, and the "Yan Can Cook" show one of the most widely viewed and longest running cooking shows in the world. And now, I am pleased to say that the "Yan Can Cook" show is being broadcast in England, the Middle East, and most of Southeast Asia, reaching millions of people with diverse cultural backgrounds and lifestyles.

In the past few years, I have had the privilege of being associated with many talented cooking professionals and had the opportunity to share the spotlight with them on various charitable occasions. I am constantly learning from the legendary Julia Child, whose mastery in the kitchen continues to amaze me. The lovable Frugal Gourmet, Jeff Smith, and his talented associate, Craig Wollam, keep me in good spirits with their creativity and enthusiasm. Nathalie Dupree and the Galloping Gourmet, Graham Kerr, provide inspiration with their friendship, talent, and love for cooking. And lastly the teacher of all teachers, Chef Jacques Pépin, who is a true professional and joy to work with on any occasion. Their conviction and knowledge continue to enrich and inspire me.

I am also grateful to have had the opportunity to work on countless projects with Joyce Jue, Gayle Yamada, Rhoda Yee, and Dr. Thomas Bloom and Chef Johnathan Robinette of the California Culinary Academy.

I am forever indebted to the talents of my producer, Linda Brandt, and director, Katherine Russell, the KQED crew, back-kitchen supervisors Tina Salter and Carl Abbott, and culinary staff, Joyce Chowla, Bernice Fong, Gladys Lee, James Leung, Vivienne Marsh, Arlene McKellar, Linda Mead, Jan Nix, Diane Onizuka, Bernie Schimbke, Joseph Strebler, and Christi Sweet for making every show an adventure and culinary masterpiece. To my staff: Virginia Bast, Deanne Dobler,

Jennifer Louie, and interns Karla Masui and Helen Soehalim; without your continued support and timeless dedication this project and many others would not have been possible.

And not to forget my partner in life Susan. This has been a roller-coaster year and the ride has only just begun. I thank you for your love, encouragement, patience and support.

I also wish to thank the following organizations and their dedicated staffs, who have generously shared their educational and informational resources, enabling us to create innovative recipes with a variety of new and exciting ingredients: California Wild Rice Program, California Prune Board, California Asparagus Commission, Monterey Mushrooms, Inc., California Artichoke Advisory Board, Dry Bean Advisory Board, California Cantaloupe Advisory Board, Texas Peanut Producers Board, Bard Valley Medjool Date Growers Association, and Grimmway Farms.

And finally, as my career moves forward, I have you, my viewers and readers, to thank for the opportunity to teach others the joy of cooking. I am most fortunate.

Contents

Introduction: The Foods of Asia

When I look back 15 years and see the very first season of the "Yan Can Cook" show and compare it to my most recent series of shows, I notice many differences. Over the years, I have demonstrated many different cooking techniques, used a variety of ingredients, and changed my approach to preparing and presenting food.

Lifestyles have also changed quite a bit in the last 15 years. People are becoming more aware of their health and its relation to food and proper eating habits. The desire for leaner meats, fresher produce, and new ethnic flavors has led to a culinary revolution, creating a fusion cuisine.

The focus of "Yan Can Cook" has always been to introduce new ways of presenting and preparing foods from around the world. It is my hope that the new "Yan Can Cook" show and its companion cookbook *The Well-Seasoned Wok* reflect the growing interest in all Asian cuisines. We have moved beyond Chinese cooking and have added recipes from many Southeast Asian cuisines, including Thailand, Singapore, Vietnam, Indonesia, and the Philippines. Southeast Asia is a melding of many countries expressing cultural and social diversity, and in many cases is influenced by the people of China. The availability of a wide range of Southeast Asian ingredients and its many cooking techniques have transformed the simplest of meals to a gourmet delight that would please any palate.

The recipes in this book are inspiring, delicious, quick, and healthy. Many of the recipes are based on my own creations. Others are favorites collected from friends and colleagues from around the world.

I hope the exciting recipes in *The Well-Seasoned Wok* will become wonderful additions to your everyday family menu. And I hope they will inspire you to create your own well-seasoned wonders. To all the friends and fans of Yan, I wish you good cooking and a happy, healthy life.

The
Asian
Kitchen

Utensils and Equipment

The selection of cooking utensils and equipment available to today's cook is truly remarkable. There's a finish, shape, and size of any piece of equipment to fit everybody's needs. You might think that to cook Asian dishes, you need a whole new set of cooking utensils and equipment. Fortunately, all you need is a few pieces of equipment to get started.

Many of the recipes in this book can be prepared with a few basic utensils—the wok, the cleaver, the steamer, and a couple of high-quality pots and pans. Maybe you've always wanted to cook your favorite Chinese dishes but were hesitant because you didn't have the traditional tools. Don't worry; while it's nice to have the many special-purpose utensils in Asian cooking, you can adapt the utensils you already own and jump right in and start cooking. When purchasing equipment, always buy high-quality pieces. After all, you want these valuable pieces of equipment to last for years to come.

The Wok

To me the wok is the most functional all-around cooking utensil. I use my wok to do everything from boiling pasta and steaming dumplings to braising meats and stir-frying my favorite seafoods. Because of its concave shape, cooking is most efficient, using a minimal amount of oil. Because cooking time is reduced, nutrients and color are retained, making wok-cooked foods full of flavor and texture.

Woks are made in a range of sizes, from as small as 9-inch diameter for home use to as large as 24 inches for restaurants. They're made from a variety of materials, including stainless steel with copper disk bottoms, hard anodized aluminum (with or without a nonstick surface), carbon steel, and even cast iron. Woks with flat and round bottoms are also available in most materials. Traditional round-bottomed woks used with ring stands work well with gas burners. Flat-bottomed woks are most efficient for those who have an electric stove because of the increased surface contact with the heating element.

Choose a wok for its efficient heating properties and its affordability, but also keep in mind that you want to choose a wok that has a size, finish, and weight that is most comfortable for you to use. Woks with nonstick surfaces are widely available in the market, and can be used right away without any treatment. If you choose a carbon steel wok, it is necessary to season the cooking surface. In the process of seasoning a wok, oil is burned into the porous surface of the metal, creating a natural nonstick surface.

To season a new rolled or hammered carbon steel wok, wash it thoroughly with soapy water to remove the oily coating used to protect the wok in transport. Wipe dry and heat over the stove top. Using a folded paper towel, rub cooking oil over the entire surface of the wok to thinly coat. With the exhaust fan on, gently heat the wok while continuously rubbing the surface with the towel, changing the towel several times, until the wok begins to darken. Carefully rotate the wok until all lower sides have come in contact with the burner. This process will take time, but after continued use your wok will have darkened and the metal aged to create a natural nonstick surface. With proper care, the seasoned surface should remain intact, protecting your food from sticking and the wok from rusting.

To clean your carbon steel wok, simply use a non-abrasive sponge and rinse in hot soapy water. Gently rub away food particles and clean the entire surface. Wipe away surface water and stove-dry your wok over high heat. Stove-drying will remove unseen moisture found in the metal pores and will help prevent future rusting. It is often recommended to rub the wok with oil before storing, but I have found this can leave an undesirable sticky coating that attracts dust, and may become rancid over time. If your wok is well seasoned and used on a regular basis, oiling your wok may not be necessary.

Seasoning can be removed from a wok if it is used repeatedly for steaming, or if an acidic mixture (such as a sweet and sour, tomato, or citrus sauce) is cooked in it for a long period of time. I would recommend that you use a stainless steel, anodized aluminum, or nonstick wok or saucepan for cooking these sauces and toss acidic foods only briefly in your well-seasoned wok.

Along with a carbon steel wok you'll get a metal spatula and ladle. The most often used utensil is the wok spatula. Its rounded corners and slightly curved bottom are designed to fit the curvature of the wok, and allow for easy tossing and stirring movements without scratching the wok's metal surface. The ladle is mainly used along with the spatula to assist in tossing motions when stir-frying. It is also used as a serving utensil transferring food from wok to serving platter. Of course, if you have a high-quality set of nonstick cookware, avoid using metal utensils. Although not as traditional as the metal wok spatula and ladle, wood or plastic versions are good alternatives.

The Chinese Chef's Knife

Aside from the wok and a few pots and pans, a good, all-purpose knife is essential. My personal preference is to have a well-balanced, lightweight knife that has an edge that is easy to maintain. Many gourmet cooks have begun to appreciate the traditionally designed Chinese chef's knife. This knife has a wide blade and while it may seem awkward to the beginner, with a few days' practice, you won't want to give it up.

Those who love to cook Asian food may want to have two Chinese chef's knives: one with a thin to medium blade, to do all of the slicing and cutting of vegetables and meats, and a heavier cleaver with a thicker blade to chop through dense bones. If you do not intend to do much chopping through bones, then a heavy cleaver is not necessary. A good thin-bladed, medium-sized, all-purpose stainless steel chef's knife will see you through most food preparations.

Through the years, I have not been able to find a high-quality Chinese chef's knife, so I decided to design my own signature high-carbon stainless steel Chinese chef's knife. This is the same knife that I use on the "Yan Can Cook" show. If you are interested in purchasing my Ultimate Chinese Chef's Knife, just drop us a note (see page 192) and we'll send you more information.

The secret of using a Chinese chef's knife is in developing confidence and coordination in handling the large blade. Part of feeling confident and comfortable involves how you hold the knife. The best way to gain control of the knife is to "choke up" on the blade as you hold the handle. Grasp the handle of the knife close to the blade and extend your index finger along one side of the blade and thumb on the other. If your fingers are totally around the handle you will have no control over the blade.

When using a Chinese chef's knife, slice in a down and forward motion; do not saw or hack. The blade cuts should be short and strokes should be shallow. The fingertips of your free hand hold the food in place. Keep them tucked under your knuckles, with the knuckles lightly touching the flat side of the blade to act as a cutting guide. The edge of the knife should never be lifted above your knuckles. The position of both your free hand and the hand holding the Chinese chef's knife will give you the ability to control the angle of the blade and maximize your force of movement.

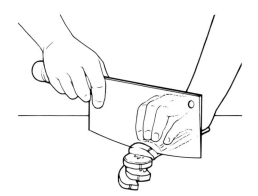

Holding the knife: Note that the fingertips of the left hand are held vertically.

The Steamer

The steamer is another useful tool to have on hand. There are basically two types of steamers available on the market, bamboo and aluminum. They come in different diameters to fit any need, whether it be for steaming small dumplings or a whole fish. Bamboo steamers are designed to sit on a wok or other pan; most aluminum steamer sets include a broad-based bottom pot to hold the water.

A typical steamer set, bamboo or aluminum, includes one or two tiers and a tight-fitting lid. Additional tiers may be stacked, allowing several different dishes or batches to be steamed at the same time. Generally, two or three tiers is the limit, because the steaming efficiency diminishes as you move upward. Food can be placed directly in the basket, or it can be lined with a variety of different materials such as cheesecloth, lettuce leaves, or soaked lotus leaves.

The bamboo steamer is preferred by Chinese chefs because excess steam can easily escape through the woven strips of bamboo. Because of this woven design, moisture cannot build up or condense on the steamer lid and drip onto the food, affecting the flavor and texture. Bamboo steamers should be washed only with hot, lightly soaped water and should be air-dried and stored in an open shelf or cupboard; storing them in an airtight place or in a plastic bag will promote mildew.

Some cooks prefer the aluminum steamer because of its durability and because it does not transfer flavors. (Bamboo steamers have a tendency to absorb and develop undesirable odors over time.) A good size of either type would be 12 inches in diameter which would accommodate any of the dishes in this book.

Collapsible steel steamers are also available and I find them to be very functional and easy to clean. A steamer can be improvised in a wok or large deep pan, using a small can opened at both ends to support the plate holding the food above the water and covering the pan with a lid. A circular cake rack also works well as a steaming rack fitted inside of a wok. No matter what type of steamer you use, the water should be filled to about ¾ inch from the bottom of the rack. This will

Three-prong steamer tong

allow the water to boil briskly without it getting into the food container and will also permit the steam to circulate freely around the food. When steaming for long periods of time, remember to replenish the water with hot water—bamboo steamers will burn if the wok becomes dry.

A handy tool to help you retrieve a hot dish is the steamer tong. There are two types available: the three-pronged lifter and the plate lifter. The three-prong gadget has a handle which, when depressed, forces its prongs open to hook around the rim of the dish. The other tool looks like a canning jar retriever, with the bottom edges bent inward. Either design allows you to lift the plate from the steamer rack without burning your hands.

The Mortar and Pestle, Mini-Processor, and Spice Grinder

Most Southeast Asian kitchens have a mortar and pestle as a basic utensil for grinding and pulverizing spices and herbs into fine seasoning pastes. The mortar is usually made from heavy stone, and is somewhat large and thick-sided. The pestle is made of the same material and is shaped like a thick rod that is slightly larger on the grinding end. Ceramic sets are also available, but the ones made of heavy stone seem to hold up best to the heavy pounding and pushing needed to produce a good spice paste.

While no other tool can quite match a mortar and pestle in extracting and releasing the flavors and aromas from spices and herbs, all that pounding and grinding is a time-consuming and laborious process. An electric spice grinder or mini-food processor does the job almost as well in a fraction of the time. A compromise that would still save some time and energy would be to process the spice mixture first in a mini-processor to produce the finest grind possible and then transfer it to a mortar and pestle to finish it off into a smoother paste.

13

Miscellaneous Tools

Other special tools of the trade in my tiny kitchen include a few clay pots for braising and stove-top casserole cooking (see page 131), long cooking chopsticks, and a wire skimmer for lifting food out of hot water or hot oil. If you are a rice eater like me, you might find a rice cooker with a "keep warm" button amazingly useful. I have two, one at home and one at my cooking school. While these tools are nice to have, they are not absolutely necessary in producing a tasty and nutritious meal. So go ahead, jump in and try any of the recipes in this book. You'll be amazed at how much you can do with whatever you have in your own kitchen.

Cooking Techniques

People often think Chinese cooking techniques are mysterious. They hear terms like stir-fry, braise, and steam and think that such techniques require a bit more skill than they have. What they don't understand is that most cooks use these techniques every day without realizing that they are doing so. To cook Asian food, you only need to know how to cut, measure, mix, and toss.

Preparation

To cook Asian food successfully you should have everything cut and measured and ready to go before you turn on the heat. At first you may not be able to cut meats and vegetables into evenly sized pieces, but with a little practice you'll soon be cutting like an expert. Combine sauces and group piles of ingredients in a logical order according to the recipe directions. Read the recipe directions before you start cooking to get an idea of what you're about to do.

Stir-Frying

This method of cooking is probably one of the most exciting and energetic ways to cook. It is called stir-frying because you must keep the food in constant motion, by stirring or tossing, to ensure even cooking. Stir-frying is usually done over high heat in a wok or wide frying pan, using a wok spatula or large spoon to keep the pieces of food moving. This fun, quick-cooking method retains natural flavors, textures, and nutrients, using very little oil.

After preparing the sauces and cutting up all the ingredients, heat the wok over high heat. Next, add the oil and the oil flavoring ingredients, such as the garlic and ginger. Most stir-frying recipes say to heat the oil in a hot wok first, then add the oil flavoring ingredients. I find that since my recipes call for very little oil, I don't need to heat the oil separately; it takes only a few seconds for the flavoring ingredients to release their flavors as the oil heats.

Once the flavoring ingredients become fragrant, the meat or seafood is added. It should be tossed rapidly in the hot oil to seal in the juices. Meats and seafood are usually removed before vegetables are added. The leftover juices will help cook and flavor the vegetables. Vegetables that are more dense or tougher in texture will be added to the hot wok next. Smaller, more fragile vegetables are added last, since they take only a short time to cook until crisp-tender. Because stir-frying takes only a few minutes, vegetables come out crisp and colorful, meats come out lightly browned and juicy.

After the vegetables are cooked, the meat is added back into the wok. A quick toss with the sauce glazes all the cooked ingredients. Lastly, a cornstarch solution is added to lightly bind all the flavors and textures together.

Braising

This is a technique commonly used to cook larger, tougher cuts of meat which benefit from longer, lower-temperature cooking. First, I heat my wok or pot with oil and lightly brown the meat to seal in the juices and give the meat a nice color. Then I add a flavoring liquid and some seasonings, tightly cover the pan, and cook in an oven or on the stovetop for several hours. The end result is always tender and succulent.

This is a good technique to use when you have something to do and want dinner to cook without your supervision. Braised dishes make great party dishes to cook ahead and reheat right before you're ready to serve.

Steaming

Because ovens aren't in every Asian household, steaming is a popular cooking technique. It is one of the most healthful ways to cook because it uses little or no added fats or oils. Steam cooking retains nutrients and brings out subtle flavors in foods. To steam, bring water to a boil in your wok or wide frying pan. Put the food in a heatproof dish and place it on a steamer rack about ¾ inch above the boiling water. Make sure your dish is of a size which will allow the steam to circulate freely. Cover the steamer with a tight-fitting lid and steam until done. If you're steaming for a long period of time, you will need to add hot or boiling water to your wok. When removing the steamer lid remember to tilt it away from you, so the escaping steam will not burn you. Use steamer tongs (see page 13) to remove hot dishes.

While steaming, it is important that you not remove the lid. Every time you remove the lid, you reduce the temperature of the steam atmosphere. If you're a peeker, add a couple of extra minutes to your cooking time.

Blanching

This technique is generally used to precook vegetables in boiling water. To blanch, bring a wok or large pot of water to a boil. Add the vegetables and cook for a few minutes. Remove the vegetables from the wok and quickly rinse with cool water to stop the cooking process. Generally vegetables are blanched only until crisp-tender or until the color turns bright.

Blanching is also used to remove the metallic taste from canned products such as mushrooms or bamboo shoots. Meats are often blanched in water to remove scum and to seal in juices before stewing.

Roasting

In China, roasting has traditionally been a restaurant technique, because most homes didn't have ovens. It's still a popular technique for Chinese restaurants and delicatessens here. Roasting meats and poultry hanging on hooks allows the hot air to circulate freely, resulting in a crisp exterior and a moist interior. To duplicate this in a home oven, place the marinated meats on a rack to raise them up off the roasting pan.

Red-Cooking

Simmering foods gently over low heat in a liquid or sauce is one of the most common cooking techniques in any cuisine. When the liquid is based on soy sauce and sugar, the technique is known as "red-cooking" because of the deep mahogany-colored glaze it gives to the food. Red-cooked meats come out tender and juicy, and the full-bodied flavor of the sauce penetrates the meat better than with any other method.

Red-cooking liquids can range from simple to complex. In addition to various types of soy sauce and water, they may contain wine, rock sugar, and seasonings such as star anise, fennel, cinnamon, five-spice, dried tangerine peel, garlic, ginger, or onions. When the liquid is strained and saved, it becomes a "master sauce" that can be used again and again. Renewed with the original ingredients and enriched with the meat juices, it becomes richer and more complex in flavor each time it is used.

To reserve a master sauce, allow it to cool and remove the fat. Refrigerate for up to a week, or freeze for longer storage. If possible, thaw the sauce overnight in the refrigerator before re-using; otherwise, melt it slowly before bringing it to a boil. Either way, simmer the sauce for at least 5 minutes before adding meat or poultry.

Deep-Frying

Cooking food in a large amount of hot oil produces a crisp golden exterior and moist interior. When it is done right, the food is never greasy. It is most important that the oil be at the right temperature. One way to test if the oil is at the proper temperature is to place the tip of a dry wooden chopstick into the bottom of the oil. If tiny bubbles emerge from the end, then your oil is ready for frying. Another easy way to test oil is to place a small bit of uncooked food into the oil; if the oil is at the right temperature, the food should immediately begin to sizzle and bubble. Of course, using an oil thermometer will immediately indicate whether or not your oil is ready for frying.

When deep-frying, it is also important that you not cook too much food at once. Cooking the food in small batches will not only allow for even cooking, but will also keep the oil at a more constant temperature throughout the cooking process. Crowding the food will cause the oil temperature to drop, making your food oily rather than crisp. Use a wire strainer or slotted spoon to remove cooked foods from the hot oil. After cooking, drain well on paper towels.

Ingredients

Many Asian ingredients that were once exotic, like bean curd, bamboo shoots, and wonton wrappers, are now found in supermarkets all over North America. Some of the more unusual ingredients used in this book are discussed here; check the Index for the location of other notes on ingredients.

Bean Curd, Fermented	Known as *fu yu* in Cantonese. Cubes of bean curd are fermented in brine for weeks and then rice wine is added to enhance flavor. Sold in jars, in either white or red varieties; the red has a stronger flavor and rich red color from red rice (page 25). Both types are used as a seasoning or as a condiment, usually pureed and mixed with other seasonings for salad dressings or stir-fry dishes.
Bean Thread Noodles	Also known as cellophane noodles or Chinese vermicelli, these thin, translucent dried noodles are made from mung bean starch. Soak them in warm water to soften them for use in soups or stir-fry dishes. For garnishing, deep-fry them right out of the package.
Black Beans, Preserved	These small black soybeans, steamed until soft, strongly salted, and then fermented, are used in a variety of dishes in many parts of China, and are a staple seasoning in Cantonese cooking. They have a pungent and salty aroma and flavor. Before using, rinse and crush the beans lightly to release their flavor. Store in an airtight jar in the refrigerator; they keep for months.
Bitter Melon	Called *foo gwa* in Cantonese, this vegetable has green, bumpy skin and resembles a wrinkled cucumber. You don't have to peel it before using, just scoop out the seeds and pulp. You may want to parboil bitter melon in salt water for a few minutes to cut down the bitterness.
Black Fungus	A small, grayish-brown dried fungus, also called "cloud ears" or "wood ears" because of their earlike shape. They need to be soaked until soft before using. Wood ears are much larger and have a firmer texture when cooked; cloud ears are smaller and softer.

| Chestnuts, Dried | These dried chestnuts from China are hard as rock and must be soaked for a couple of hours and then cooked before they are soft enough to be served. Cooked, they have a pleasant crunchiness and sweetness. Available in most Asian stores. |

Chestnuts, Dried — These dried chestnuts from China are hard as rock and must be soaked for a couple of hours and then cooked before they are soft enough to be served. Cooked, they have a pleasant crunchiness and sweetness. Available in most Asian stores.

Chiles — There are many varieties of chiles used in Chinese and Southeast Asian cuisine. For fresh chiles, I generally specify serranos or jalapeños because they are widely available; but you can substitute other fresh varieties. Fresh chiles keep best in the refrigerator, wrapped in a paper towel inside a plastic bag.

Many recipes call for "small dried red chiles." These are the ripened and dried version of serranos or other small chiles, sold in most spice sections but much cheaper in Asian markets.

Chili Pastes and Sauces — A wide variety of bottled or canned pastes made from fresh or dried chiles are available on the market. Some brands contain black beans, while others have lots of garlic. Each brand differs in intensity and flavor profile, so adjust recipe amounts accordingly. *Sweet chili sauce* is a thinner, sweeter Thai variety sold in tall bottles, sometimes labeled "for chicken."

Chinese Chives — Large, flat Chinese chives come in two varieties, green and yellow. The darker green variety, also known as garlic chive, is a little stronger and sweeter than regular chives; it's mostly used in fillings for dim sum or with scrambled eggs. The yellow chive, with its milder, sweet-onion flavor, is usually used in soups.

Coconut Milk — Perhaps the most widely used ingredient in all of Southeast Asian cooking, coconut milk is not the liquid found inside the coconut, but a rich liquid extracted from the grated meat. It is often used as a substitute for dairy cream in Asian desserts and sauces. You can make your own from a fresh coconut, but canned coconut milk from Southeast Asia is available in most Asian stores and is much more convenient.

If a recipe calls for coconut cream, do not shake the can before opening, and spoon the thick cream off the top. Otherwise, shake the can vigorously before opening to blend the cream and the thinner milk. When cooking with coconut milk, cook over medium to low heat and stir slowly and frequently to prevent curdling. Leftover coconut milk can be kept in the refrigerator for about 2 days, or can be frozen.

Daikon

A large, cylindrical white radish, up to 1½ feet long and 2 inches or more in diameter. Also known as the Chinese white turnip or Korean turnip. With a mildly sweet taste as radishes go, it is one of the most widely used vegetables in Japanese cuisine, and a favorite in Chinese cooking as well. The Chinese variety is shorter, thicker, and more fibrous, with a stronger flavor than the Japanese. *Pickled radish strips* are a salted and preserved form of daikon, sold in packages in Asian markets; they have a salty, sour taste and a crunchy texture.

Eggplant, Asian

Much smaller in diameter than regular eggplant with glossy, dark purple skin, and fewer seeds. It is similar in texture and cooking qualities to regular eggplant, but sweeter in taste.

Fish Sauce

An aromatic amber liquid extract of salted fish, used throughout Southeast Asia as soy sauce is in China and Japan. Most of the brands sold here are imported from Thailand.

Five-Spice, Chinese   An all-purpose seasoning made from a blend of five or more ground spices, usually star anise or anise seeds, cloves, cinnamon, fennel, and Sichuan peppercorns. Most marinades for Cantonese barbecued meats use five-spice powder. It may be found in small bottles or plastic bags in supermarkets or Asian stores.

Fuzzy Melon   Also known as hairy melon or fuzzy squash, or *jit gwa* in Cantonese, fuzzy melon comes in two shapes, both with apple-green skin covered with very short bristly 'hairs." The long variety grows to 10 or 12 inches and 2 to 3 inches in diameter; the shorter oval variety resembles a small watermelon, 4 to 6 inches long and about 3 inches in diameter. The hairy skin should be removed before cooking. The flavor is not sweet like other melons, but more like mild squash or cucumber.

Galangal   This root, a relative of ginger, is sold fresh, in dried slices, or as a powder. It has a fiery hot taste, and is an important ingredient in Thai curry pastes. The dried, sliced root must be soaked before using. Galangal is only available in Asian stores.

Hoisin Sauce   A sweet, tangy, thick, dark brown sauce made from fermented soybeans and flavored with vinegar, sugar, garlic, and spices. It is used as a barbecue sauce, condiment, or seasoning sauce in meat dishes. Available in cans or jars. Refrigerate after opening.

Jasmine Rice   See Rice, Long-Grain

Kaffir Lime Rind   The green, crinkled rind of a Southeast Asian citrus fruit, sold dried in thick shreds in Asian stores. It must be soaked until soft before being minced or ground into curry pastes and other dishes.

Lemongrass

A popular seasoning in Southeast Asian cooking, this long, fibrous, yellow-green grasslike stalk imparts subtle lemon flavor to curries, soups, and simmered dishes. Only the bottom 6 to 8 inches are tender enough to slice, chop, or pound to a paste in a mortar. Choose stalks which feel solid inside when squeezed near the root end, not spongy, loose, or dried out. Fresh stalks are preferable, but dried lemongrass is also available. Store fresh stalks in plastic wrap in the refrigerator for up to two weeks.

Lily Buds, Dried

These dried, unopened flower buds of yellow and orange day lilies are known in China as *gum jump*. The buds are about 2½ to 3 inches in length and have a slightly velvety texture, and a sweet, yet earthy fragrance. They should be soaked in warm water until softened and the hard stem ends should be removed before using. Sold in plastic packages in Asian stores.

Lumpia Wrappers

The Filipino name for very thin square or round sheets made of flour, egg, and cornstarch, similar to Chinese spring roll wrappers. Lumpia wrappers are thinner and paler than egg roll wrappers, and give a crisper texture than egg roll wrappers when deep-fried. Sold refrigerated or frozen in plastic packages in Asian stores.

Lychee

This bright brick- and crimson-colored tropical fruit, originally from southern China, has a bumpy, leathery skin encasing a delicious juicy white fruit with a dark hard seed in the center. The white meat is translucent white and sweet with a texture similar to a soft

23

juicy grape. Lychees are commonly canned in light syrup, but try them fresh when they appear in Chinese markets in early summer.

Mirin	A sweetened, golden-colored Japanese rice wine used only for cooking. Since it has a high sugar content, it is often used in sauces for teriyaki or sukiyaki dishes.

Miso

A thick protein-rich paste made from ground fermented soy beans. Miso comes in several types and flavors, the lighter versions generally milder and sweeter than the darker ones. Sold in tubs and plastic packs, labelled by color (red, brown, yellow, and white or light). It will keep in the refrigerator for a month.

Mushrooms

In addition to the common commercial button mushrooms, I use a variety of fresh, canned, and dried mushrooms. One of my favorite fresh varieties is the *oyster mushroom,* so called because its gray-beige colored cap and subtle seafood flavor remind us of oysters. This mushroom grows on dead trees and has been cultivated in Asia for centuries, and it is now available in most supermarkets here. It can be stir-fried, grilled, or deep-fried.

Enoki mushrooms are tiny and white, with 1/8- to 1/4-inch caps and very thin stems. They are used in soups and other dishes for their delicate flavor and texture. The mushrooms grow in clumps attached at the bottom, and are sold that way in plastic bags in supermarkets and Asian food stores. The bottom attached area of the growth clump should be cut off and discarded. Enokis do not keep very long and should be used as soon as they are purchased.

Dried black mushrooms, also known by their Japanese name *shiitake,* have wide, flat caps, a rich, meaty flavor and texture, and a distinctive, pleasant aroma. Better-quality ones have a lacy system of cracks on the surface of the cap and a creamy-colored underside. To use, soak in water for 30 minutes until softened and discard the stems. *Fresh shiitakes* are available in most supermarkets, but do not have the same distinctive flavor and meaty texture as the dried ones.

Straw mushrooms are available only in cans from Asia. Light brown in color, they resemble partially opened umbrellas with sturdy straw-colored stems. They have a delicate sweetness and a tender, slightly crunchy texture. Available "peeled," that is, with the cap opened; but most Chinese chefs prefer the "unpeeled" type in which the cap completely covers the stem.

Plum Sauce, Chinese	A rich golden sauce with a jam-like consistency and a spicy, sweet, and tangy flavor, made from salted plums, yam puree, rice vinegar, sugar, and chile. Different brands vary in thickness and intensity of flavor. Available in cans and jars; keeps indefinitely in the refrigerator.
Potato Starch	Also referred to as potato flour. Potato starch is commonly used in Southeast Asia as a thickener because it binds better than cornstarch. The Japanese variety of cellophane noodles (*saifun*) are made with potato starch. Sold in plastic bags in Asian stores.
Radish Strips, Pickled	See Daikon.
Red Rice	Uncooked rice infused with a natural red by-product of rice wine production, also called red yeast, red wine lees, or *heung gok mai* in Chinese. Although it does not have a lot of taste, red rice is used to impart a lovely red color to slow-simmered dishes, and it's also

an ingredient in some prepared sauces, such as hoisin sauce. It is sold in Asian markets and Chinese herbal shops, either dry or in jars with liquid. Only a small amount is needed to add color.

Rice

Rice is one of the most basic foods in Asia, common to nearly all Asian cuisines. There are lots of varieties, several of which are used in this book:

Long-grain white rice is the everyday rice preferred by most Chinese. When properly cooked, it's drier and less sticky than shorter varieties, and the grains separate and fluff easily with a chopstick or fork. This is definitely the best type to use for fried rice dishes.

Jasmine rice is a fragrant long-grain variety grown in many parts of Thailand. It is richly aromatic with slender, long grains and is similar to basmati rice in appearance and aroma. This rice usually needs no added flavorings and is served like regular rice.

Basmati rice is another highly aromatic variety grown in India, with especially long, curved grains. It is aged for one year to develop its unique nutty flavor. Basmati, available either white or brown, is good with curries and in salads and other rice dishes. Texmati is another form of basmati rice grown in Texas.

Glutinous rice is an entirely different variety, also known as sweet or sticky rice because of its texture when cooked. The short grains are opaque white when raw and become translucent after cooking (the opposite of other varieties). Glutinous rice requires less water in cooking than long-grain rice. It is used in both sweet and savory dishes, including dumplings, stuffings, and desserts.

Before cooking all varieties of rice, I rinse the grains in several changes of water, draining well each time.

Rice Vinegar

Vinegars made from the fermentation of rice can be

white, slightly yellowish, or dark. All rice vinegar varieties are less acidic than distilled white vinegar, and have a full-bodied, pleasant aroma. Japanese cooks often use a kind of rice vinegar preseasoned with sugar, mainly for preparing sushi rice. Unless this variety is specified, use the unseasoned variety. White rice vinegar can be used like any white or red wine vinegar in cooking or salad dressings.

Chinese dark rice vinegar has a rich brown color and a full-bodied, almost sweet caramel flavor. One popular example is Chinkiang vinegar from eastern China. Balsamic vinegar is a good substitute.

Sake

A Japanese wine made from fermented rice, used both as a beverage and in cooking. In cooking, it is normally used along with soy sauce and sugar, and it adds a unique flavor to many popular Japanese dishes such as teriyaki and sukiyaki. Sake is readily available in most supermarkets. It's perishable, and for best flavor it should be used within a year of manufacture.

Sesame Oil

Asian-style sesame oil is a deep brown and aromatic oil pressed from toasted sesame seeds. It is used mainly as a flavoring agent. Look for 100 percent pure sesame oil; some brands are blended with soybean oil, reducing the favorable flavor characteristics. Only a small amount is needed to flavor any dish. Add sesame oil during the last few seconds of cooking, as excessive heating will destroy its unique flavor. Keep refrigerated after opening.

Shao Hsing Wine

China's most famous wine, made from a fermented blend of glutinous rice, millet, and special yeast which is aged for 10 years. As a beverage, it is served chilled or warm. It has a very similar color, taste, and alcohol content to dry sherry. It is used mostly in northern Chinese cooking, and is mainly available in Asian stores. Dry sherry is an adequate substitute.

Shrimp, Dried

Small shrimp preserved in brine and then dried in the sun. Used sparingly, they give a pronounced salt-fish flavor to vegetable dishes and soups. Sold in plastic bags in Asian stores. Look for plump shrimp with a bright pink-orange color, not gray or brownish and not shriveled up. Soak dried shrimp in warm water for 30 minutes to soften before using. Store dried shrimp in the refrigerator in an airtight container.

Shrimp Paste

A fragrant seasoning paste made from ground, salted, and fermented shrimp. There are two kinds of paste: one is dry, firm, and has a dark brownish color and pungent smell; the other is also dry in texture, milder, and softer with a shrimp-pink color. Both are widely used in a variety of Asian dishes and are essential in authentic Thai and Vietnamese cooking. This is one seasoning that you need to develop a taste for. Store in an airtight sealed jar.

Sichuan Peppercorns

Not really peppercorns, but tiny red-brown dried berries with a pungent aroma and pleasant numbing flavor. To bring out their distinctive flavor, toast in a frying pan over medium to medium-low heat for about 5 minutes until fragrant, stirring or shaking the pan frequently to prevent burning. Then grind the toasted peppercorns with a mortar and pestle or spice grinder. Keep in an airtight jar. Whole and ground Sichuan peppercorns are available in small packages and jars in Asian markets and specialty gourmet stores.

Sichuan Preserved Vegetable	This hot and spicy pickled radish or kohlrabi, called *jah choy* in Cantonese, is used in a variety of dishes in Sichuan and northern China. Sold in cans or plastic bags or from large earthenware pickling crocks in Asian stores. To cut down on the saltiness and strong flavor, let it soak in fresh water for a while, or at least rinse off some of the chile powder and salt.
Soy Sauce	An essential seasoning ingredient in Chinese and Japanese cooking, with a wide range in saltiness and sweetness. Unless otherwise specified, use the regular variety soy sauce available in the supermarket. *Dark soy sauce* is exclusively Chinese; an addition of molasses makes it thicker, darker, and sweeter, imparting a smoky-caramel flavor. It is used when a richer, deeper color and flavor are desired in stews and casseroles. *Thin soy sauce* is thinner, saltier, and lighter in color and flavor than regular soy sauce; it is not to be confused with *light soy sauce,* which is a reduced-sodium regular soy sauce. Select only a naturally fermented brand, like Kikkoman; some supermarket brands are chemically hydrolyzed, and are not recommended.
Star Anise	A shiny mahogany-colored seed pod with an eight-pointed star shape. Whole or ground, the pods and the shiny seeds they contain provide a distinctively strong licorice flavor to stews, barbecues, and meats to be served cold. They are sold in Asian markets in plastic bags of various size.
Sweet Bean Sauce	This sweet, slightly spicy and pungent sauce, made from a mixture of pureed fermented soybeans, sugar, and chiles, is used as a flavoring sauce in many Sichuan and northern Chinese dishes. Do not confuse this with the sweetened red bean paste made from red azuki beans.

Tangerine Peel, Dried

Sun-dried tangerine peel is used in soups or stewed dishes to give a pungent, sweet, delightfully citrusy aroma. Store in an airtight jar, and soak to soften before using. Fresh orange or lemon peel may be substituted.

Thai Basil

Also known as Asian basil or licorice basil. This herb has small green leaves and purple stems, and a flavor that combines basil and anise. May be used in salads, stir-fried dishes, and curries. Usually found in Asian stores. It's as easy as other forms of basil to grow at home.

Udon Noodles

Thick white Japanese noodles, similar to spaghetti, made from wheat flour, salt, and water. May be round or flat and are usually served in soup or broth. May be found dried or fresh in Asian stores.

Water Chestnuts

Most water chestnuts are sold canned, but if you find them fresh, by all means try them. When fresh, they have a delicate sweetness like that of fresh coconut. Choose firm ones free of wrinkles and mold. Unpeeled, they will keep up to 2 weeks in a paper bag in the refrigerator. Peel just before using and place in water to prevent discoloration. You can also freeze whole peeled water chestnuts in a sealable plastic bag; thaw them as needed and cut while still slightly frozen.

White Fungus, Dried

Also known as snow fungus, this dried, crunchy fungus resembles a golden, crinkly sponge which turns silver after soaking. It has little flavor of its own, but it adds texture to savory dishes and sweet dessert soups and readily absorbs the flavors of other ingredients present. Sold only in Asian stores.

Appetizers
and
Soups

Curried Beef Pastries

Dough

2⅔ cups all-purpose flour
1 teaspoon salt
½ cup cold shortening or lard
½ cup cold unsalted butter
6 tablespoons ice water

Filling

1 tablespoon cooking oil
2 tablespoons finely chopped onion
1 teaspoon minced ginger
⅓ cup finely chopped water chestnuts
2 tablespoons chopped cilantro or green onion
2 tablespoons oyster sauce
1 tablespoon *each* dry sherry and soy sauce
1 tablespoon curry powder
¼ teaspoon Chinese five-spice
½ pound lean ground beef
2 teaspoons cornstarch

❀

2 egg yolks, beaten with 1 teaspoon water

A quick "zip" of the food processor and a quicker wok saute are the tricks behind this savory pastry. The curry-flavored beef filling studded with chopped water chestnuts adds extra crunch. Served hot or at room temperature, it will be a sure hit at your next cocktail party.

Makes about 48

1. Place the flour and salt in a food processor and process for 2 seconds. Cut the shortening and butter into ½-inch chunks and scatter over the flour. Process until the fat particles look like small peas, 6 to 8 seconds. With the motor running, add the ice water through the feed tube. Process just until the mixture is crumbly. Remove from the processor and press together into a ball. Cut the dough into 4 pieces and wrap each in plastic wrap. Chill for 1 hour.

2. Prepare the filling: Heat a wok over high heat until hot. Add the oil, onion, and ginger and stir-fry for 1 minute. Add the water chestnuts, cilantro, oyster sauce, sherry, soy sauce, curry powder, and five-spice; cook for 45 seconds. Turn off the heat. Add the beef and mix well. Stir in the cornstarch. Remove from the heat, transfer to a bowl, and let cool.

3. Preheat the oven to 425°F. On a lightly floured board, roll out 1 piece of dough at a time into a circle ¼ inch thick. Cut out 3-inch rounds with a fluted pastry cutter. Place 1 teaspoon of the filling slightly off center on each round. Brush the edges with water, fold the dough over to make half moons, and press the edges to seal. Cut 2 or 3 slits in the top of each pastry. Place the pastries on a parchment-lined or greased baking sheet. Brush the pastries with egg wash. Bake until the pastries are golden brown, 10 to 12 minutes.

Inari Zushi

4 dried black mushrooms
½ cup water
2 tablespoons soy sauce
2 tablespoons mirin (Japanese
   sweet rice wine)
¼ cup finely diced carrot
¼ cup finely chopped green
   beans
1 tablespoon toasted sesame
   seeds (see page 78)

Sushi Rice
2 tablespoons rice vinegar
1½ tablespoons sugar
¼ teaspoon salt
1½ cups medium-grain rice
2 cups water

✿

1 can (about 10 ounces)
   Japanese fried bean curd

The idea of rolling cooked rice into little balls originated in China, perhaps thousands of years ago; but it took the imagination of Japanese cooks to turn this simple snack into dozens of beautiful, mouth-watering delicacies known as sushi. In this version, sushi rice is stuffed in a pouch of seasoned fried tofu. It tastes slightly sweet and tangy and makes great picnic food. Look for cans of ready-to-stuff seasoned fried bean curd in Asian markets. It also goes by the name of *age* or *aburage*.

Makes about 18

1. Soak the mushrooms in warm water for 30 minutes; drain. Discard the stems. In a small pan, bring the water, soy sauce, and mirin to a boil. Add the mushrooms and simmer over medium heat for 5 minutes; drain. Dice the mushrooms. Blanch the carrot and green beans in boiling water for 1 minute. Drain, rinse with cold water, and drain again.

2. Prepare the rice: In a small pan, heat the vinegar, sugar, and salt over low heat until the sugar dissolves; cool. In a covered 2-quart pan, bring the rice and water to a boil. Reduce the heat and simmer for 20 minutes or until the liquid evaporates.

3. Place the hot rice in a shallow pan. Pour the vinegar mixture over the rice and fold in the liquid with a rice paddle or spatula. Fold in the mushrooms, carrot, green beans, and sesame seeds.

4. Gently open the bean curd pouches and stuff with sushi rice. For an appetizer, fill each pouch half-full and fold the top over to enclose. For a heartier snack, stuff each pouch to the brim. If you have leftover sushi rice, shape it into walnut-size balls and serve alongside the *inari zushi*. Serve at room temperature.

TIPS: To bring out the luster of the rice, fan it while folding in the rice vinegar mixture. Any item that moves the air will work — a fan, a paper plate, or a folded newspaper.

Sushi is usually made from slightly sticky medium-grain rice. To keep the rice from sticking to your hands when you work, dip your fingers in a bowl of vinegar-water. Because the rice gets hard if stored in the refrigerator for too long, it's best to prepare the rice and fill the pouches only a few hours ahead. Cover and let stand at room temperature until serving time.

Pearl Balls

1 cup glutinous rice
1½ pounds finely chopped or ground lean pork
¼ cup minced Sichuan preserved vegetable
¼ cup chopped water chestnuts
2 tablespoons soy sauce
1 egg, lightly beaten
1 tablespoon chopped green onion or cilantro
2 teaspoons minced ginger
½ teaspoon *each* salt and white pepper
1 teaspoon sesame oil

If you've ever eaten glutinous rice, you may recall its sticky, soft texture and slightly sweet flavor. In this classic dim sum dish, glutinous rice coats juicy steamed pork balls, giving the appearance of translucent pearls. Try these tasty delights and you'll see what I mean.

Makes 24

1. Place the rice in a bowl, cover with cold water, and let stand overnight; drain. Spread the rice on a plate.

2. Place the remaining ingredients in a large bowl; mix well. With wet hands, roll the meat mixture into 24 equal balls, about 2 tablespoons each. Roll each ball in the rice to coat completely. Arrange the meatballs, without crowding, on two heatproof glass pie plates.

3. Set one dish on a rack in a steamer, cover, and steam until the pork is cooked through, about 25 minutes. Add water as needed. Serve the first portion while you steam the second.

TIP: Glutinous rice cooks up moist and sticky; long-grain rice cooks up dry with grains separate and individual. Because of the different cooked textures, long-grain rice cannot be used as a substitute in this recipe.

Fire and Ice Squid

Dipping Sauce

¼ cup chicken broth
3 tablespoons soy sauce
3 tablespoons Chinese dark
    rice vinegar
2 jalapeño or serrano chiles,
    thinly sliced
1 tablespoon chopped
    cilantro
1 tablespoon sugar
1½ teaspoons grated ginger
✿
2 pounds small squid, cleaned

Poaching Liquid

6 cups water
2 thin slices ginger, lightly
    crushed
1 green onion, cut in half
1 teaspoon salt
✿
1 teaspoon cornstarch
½ teaspoon salt
2 cups panko (Japanese-style
    bread crumbs)
¼ cup sesame seeds
Cornstarch for dry-coating
2 eggs, lightly beaten with 1
    teaspoon water
Cooking oil for deep-frying

Some people like squid fried with a crispy coating, others think poached squid is best. To please both camps, and to doubly tempt guests, serve the two styles of squid together, and let your guests choose. You'll find the spicy Thai-style dipping sauce is delicious with both.

Serves 8

1. Combine the sauce ingredients in a small bowl, stirring to dissolve the sugar. Cover and chill.

2. Slit open the squid hoods and lightly score them diagonally with crosshatching marks ½ inch apart. Cut in roughly 2-inch squares; leave the tentacles whole.

3. Bring the poaching liquid ingredients to a boil in a medium pot. Add half of the squid (including half of the tentacles), and cook for 30 seconds. Drain, rinse with cold water, and drain again. Cover and chill until ready to serve.

4. Sprinkle the remaining squid with the cornstarch and salt. Mix the panko and sesame seeds together on a plate. Dredge the squid in cornstarch. Dip each piece in the egg, drain briefly, then coat with the panko mixture. Heat the oil over medium-high heat to 375°F. Deep-fry the squid, a portion at a time, until golden and crisp, 1 to 2 minutes. Lift out and drain on paper towels.

5. To serve, place the dipping sauce in the center of a serving plate. Arrange the poached squid on one side of the plate; place the fried squid on the opposite side.

TIP: Many fish markets sell small squid already cleaned. To do it yourself, place the squid on a cutting surface; remove the head and tentacles by cutting between the eyes and body. Cut off and discard the section with the eyes, leaving the tentacles intact; remove the hard beak in the center of the tentacles. Remove the entrails from the cavity, pulling out the clear plastic-looking quill. Pull off the speckled skin from the body and discard. Rinse thoroughly with water and drain.

Vegetable Potsticker Buns

Filling
4 dried black mushrooms
4 cups finely chopped
    cabbage
½ teaspoon salt
1 tablespoon cooking oil
1 teaspoon *each* minced garlic
    and ginger
½ cup diced bamboo shoots
½ cup chopped fresh button
    mushrooms
¼ cup diced carrot
2 tablespoons soy sauce
1 teaspoon sugar
½ teaspoon white pepper
1 teaspoon sesame oil
3 green onions, thinly sliced
2 tablespoons cornstarch
    dissolved in 2
    tablespoons water

Dough
1 package (2 teaspoons)
    active dry yeast
¼ cup warm water (110°F)
¼ cup warm milk
2 cups all-purpose flour
2 tablespoons sugar
2 tablespoons shortening
✿
2 tablespoons cooking oil
1 cup chicken broth
2 teaspoons sesame oil

Steaming is the traditional way to cook these savory pastries, but they are even more juicy when cooked by a technique I call the potsticker technique. First, brown the bottoms of the buns in a little oil, then when they are golden, add broth, cover, and pan-steam until the buns are puffy and light. Delicious.

Makes 24

1. Prepare the filling: Soak the mushrooms in warm water for 30 minutes; drain. Discard the stems and finely dice the caps. Sprinkle the cabbage with salt and let stand for 30 minutes; squeeze to extract any moisture.

2. Heat a wok over high heat until hot. Add the cooking oil, garlic, and ginger and stir-fry for 10 seconds. Add the diced mushrooms, cabbage, bamboo shoots, fresh mushrooms, and carrot and stir-fry for 1½ minutes. Add the soy sauce, sugar, pepper, and sesame oil and cook for 2 minutes. Add the green onions and corn-starch solution and cook, stirring continuously, until very thick, about 1 minute. Transfer to a bowl, let cool, then chill for at least 1 hour.

3. Prepare the dough: In a large bowl, dissolve the yeast in the water. Let stand until bubbly, about 10 minutes. Gradually mix in the milk, flour, sugar, and shortening. Add 1 or 2 tablespoons more water if the dough is crumbly. On a lightly floured board, knead the dough until smooth and elastic, about 5 minutes. Shape into a ball and place in a greased bowl; turn the dough over to grease the top. Cover with a damp cloth and let rise in a warm place until doubled, about 1 hour. Punch down the dough and shape it into a ball. Cover with a damp cloth and let rest for 10 to 15 minutes.

4. On a lightly floured board, roll the dough into a 12-inch-long cylinder. Cut the cylinder in half, then cut each half into 12 pieces. Roll each piece into a ball. Flatten one ball with a rolling pin to make a 3- to 3½-

inch circle; keep the remaining dough covered to prevent drying. Place 1 heaping teaspoon of the filling in the center of the circle. Gather the edges of the circle over the filling, and close the top by pleating, then twisting the pleated edges together. Place the buns seam side up in a lightly floured shallow pan and let them rise for 5 to 10 minutes.

5. Cook the buns a dozen at a time. For each batch, heat 1 tablespoon cooking oil in a heavy, wide nonstick frying pan over medium heat. Set the buns seam side up in the pan and cook until the bottoms are golden brown, about 2 minutes. Pour ½ cup broth into the pan, around but not on the buns, and immediately cover the pan tightly. Reduce the heat to medium-low and cook for 6 minutes. Uncover and continue cooking until all the liquid is absorbed. Drizzle 1 teaspoon sesame oil around the buns and cook for 1 more minute or until the bottoms of the buns are dried.

Crispy Seafood Triangles

Filling

2 cans (6½ ounces each) chopped clams
6 ounces cream cheese
2 tablespoons chopped cilantro
1 jalapeño or serrano chile, minced
1 teaspoon lemon juice
1 teaspoon sesame oil
¼ teaspoon black pepper

✿

If you ordered this popular appetizer in a Chinese restaurant in the American Midwest, chances are it would be called Seafood Crab Puff or Fried Seafood Wonton and the filling would be made with crab. I chose a different angle for my triangles by filling them with chopped clams, cream cheese, jalapeño chile, and cilantro. Take a bite of my crispy flaky triangles and you'll find a creamy treasure of goodies inside.

Makes 24

1. Prepare the filling: Drain the clams; save the clam juice for other purposes. In a medium bowl, beat the cream cheese until soft. Stir in the clams and remaining filling ingredients; mix well.

1 dozen spring roll or lumpia
    wrappers *or* 2 dozen
    wonton skins (see Tip)
1 egg white, lightly beaten
Cooking oil for deep-frying

2. If using spring roll or lumpia wrappers, cut them into strips, each about 3 inches by 7 inches. For each triangle place a rounded teaspoon of the filling on one short end of a strip; keep the remaining wrappers covered to prevent drying. Fold over one corner to make a triangle. Fold the triangle over again on itself. Continue folding, from side to side, as if you were folding a flag. Brush the edges of the final fold with the egg white and press to seal. Place the filled triangles slightly apart on a baking sheet and cover with a cloth while you fill the remaining wrappers.

3. Heat the oil over medium-high heat to 350°F. Deep-fry the triangles, a few at a time, turning continuously to brown evenly, until golden brown, about 1 minute. Lift out and drain on paper towels.

4. Arrange the appetizers in a basket or on a tray lined with a ti leaf or banana leaf. Serve hot.

TIP: If you cannot find spring roll wrappers, use wonton skins. (Egg roll wrappers, though similar in size to spring roll wrappers, are too thick to use for this purpose.) To use wonton skins, place a rounded teaspoon of the filling in the center of a wrapper, brush the edges lightly with egg white, fold it in half over the filling to form a triangle, and press the edges firmly to seal.

Chopsticks are recognized worldwide as a symbol of Chinese and Japanese food. They also have their own fascinating history and traditions. Look for this symbol (the Chinese characters for chopsticks) to mark bits of chopstick lore here and there throughout the book.

Chicken Satay with Peanut Sauce

Marinade

¼ cup soy sauce
2 tablespoons cooking oil
1 tablespoon lemon juice
1 tablespoon curry powder
1 tablespoon sugar
1 teaspoon *each* ground
  cumin and ground
  coriander
¼ teaspoon Chinese
  five-spice

✿

1½ pounds boneless, skinless
  chicken, cut into long
  thin strips
12 (8- to 10-inch) bamboo
  skewers

Peanut Sauce

1 cup dry-roasted peanuts
½ cup coconut milk
2 tablespoons lemon juice
1½ tablespoons (packed)
  brown sugar
1 tablespoon kecap manis
  (Indonesian soy sauce)
1 to 1½ teaspoons Chinese
  chili sauce (to taste)
2 teaspoons cooking oil
2 tablespoons finely chopped
  onion
2 teaspoons minced garlic

In Southeast Asia one can taste a dozen versions of satay—tasty morsels of beef, pork, lamb, or chicken grilled on bamboo skewers. Some cooks say the flavor secret is in the marinade; others build their reputation on their master grilling techniques, cooking over hot coals to give that characteristic charcoal flavor and burnished finish. All satay cooks agree on one thing: you need a good peanut dipping sauce.

Makes 12

1. Combine the marinade ingredients in a medium bowl and whisk to dissolve the sugar and blend the spices. Add the chicken and stir to coat. Cover and refrigerate for 1 hour. Soak the bamboo skewers in water while the chicken marinates.

2. Prepare the peanut sauce: In a food processor, process the peanuts until the puree is smooth and forms a ball. Add the coconut milk, lemon juice, brown sugar, kecap manis, and chili sauce; process until smooth. Heat a 2-quart pan over medium heat until hot. Add the oil, onion, and garlic and cook for 2 minutes. Stir in the peanut mixture and heat through. Do not allow the sauce to boil. The sauce should be the consistency of heavy cream; if it becomes too thick, stir in 1 to 2 tablespoons of hot water. Set the sauce aside; just before serving, reheat over low heat.

3. Lift the chicken from the marinade; reserve the marinade. Weave the chicken strips accordion fashion on skewers; leave 2 inches uncovered at the base of each skewer to serve as a handle.

4. Place the skewers on an oiled grill over a solid bed of glowing coals. Grill, basting once with the reserved marinade, until richly browned, 2 to 3 minutes on each side. Serve with the peanut sauce on the side.

TIP: If you don't have dry-roasted peanuts on hand, use ⅔ cup peanut butter as a substitute. Personally, my favorite peanuts are the small, red-skinned Spanish variety and the runner type of cocktail peanuts grown in Texas. They have great texture and flavor, both for cooking and snacking. What's more, they are an excellent source of protein, fiber, and B vitamins.

Tortilla Rollups

Cheese Spread

1 package (8 ounces) cream cheese, softened
2 tablespoons sweet chili sauce
2 tablespoons lemon juice
1 teaspoon Worcestershire sauce
2 tablespoons chopped cilantro
1 teaspoon grated ginger
½ teaspoon minced garlic
½ teaspoon *each* salt and white pepper
✿
4 large flour tortillas (10-inch diameter)
½ pound Chinese barbecued pork, thinly sliced
¼ pound fresh shiitake or fresh button mushrooms, thinly sliced
1 cucumber, peeled, seeded, and thinly sliced
½ medium red onion, thinly sliced
20 large fresh basil leaves, julienned

This appetizer is as easy as 1-2-3: Spread seasoned cream cheese on a flour tortilla, top it with my secret ingredients, and roll it up. Presto! A great appetizer or snack for your next get-together.

Makes 16

1. Prepare the cheese spread: With a wooden spatula or electric mixer, beat the cream cheese, chili sauce, lemon juice, and Worcestershire sauce in a medium bowl until light and fluffy. Add the remaning cheese spread ingredients; mix well.

2. With wet hands, lightly moisten both sides of a tortilla. Spread ¼ of the cheese mixture to within 1 inch of the edge. Evenly layer ¼ of the pork, mushrooms, cucumber, onion, and basil on top. Roll up and wrap with plastic wrap, twisting the ends to seal. Repeat to make 3 more roll-ups. Refrigerate for at least 1 hour or up to 8 hours.

3. To serve, trim ½ inch from the ends of each roll and cut diagonally into 4 slices.

Wonton Chips with Red Pepper Salsa

Who says chips have to be made from potatoes or corn? Next time you get a craving for chips and salsa, try these, made from quick-fried wonton wrappers, and dip them in a savory salsa made from roasted red bell peppers. They're both easy to make and incredibly delicious.

Serves 8 to 10

Roasted Sweet Pepper Salsa

2 large tomatoes, cored and finely diced
1 large red bell pepper, roasted, peeled, seeded, and finely diced (about ½ cup)
2 or 3 jalapeño or serrano chiles, minced
¼ cup chopped cilantro
2 tablespoons finely chopped pickled ginger
1 teaspoon minced garlic
2 tablespoons rice vinegar
1 tablespoon Chinese chili sauce

✿

2 teaspoons salt
1 teaspoon ground toasted Sichuan peppercorns (see page 28)
1 package (1 pound) wonton skins
Cooking oil for deep-frying

1. Combine the salsa ingredients in a medium bowl; mix well. Place in a serving bowl, cover, and refrigerate until ready to use.

2. Mix the salt and Sichuan peppercorns in a small bowl; set aside. Cut the wonton skins in half diagonally to make triangles.

3. Heat the oil over medium-high heat to 360°F. Deep-fry the wonton triangles, a few at a time, until lightly browned, 15 to 20 seconds on each side. Lift out and drain on paper towels. While the chips are still hot, sprinkle lightly with the salt-peppercorn mixture.

4. Serve the chips in a basket. Offer the salsa alongside for dipping.

TIP: You could use raw bell pepper in this salsa, but roasting the peppers first brings out a delicious sweet, smoky flavor. A quick method is to place bell peppers (red or green) in a shallow pan and broil 3 inches from the heat until blistered and charred on all sides. Transfer the peppers to a paper bag or covered pan and let stand for 10 to 15 minutes, then peel, seed, and use as directed. You can also buy roasted and peeled red peppers in jars.

Wonton Chips with Red Pepper Salsa and Tortilla Rollups (page 41)

Oysters on the Half Shell

Black Bean Sauce
2 teaspoons cooking oil
2 teaspoons minced garlic
2 teaspoons minced ginger
1 tablespoon salted black
    beans, rinsed, drained,
    and coarsely chopped
2 tablespoons chicken broth
1 tablespoon soy sauce
2 teaspoons minced green
    onion
1 teaspoon sesame oil
½ teaspoon sugar

Garlic Butter
1 tablespoon butter
1 tablespoon *each* minced
    garlic and shallot
2 teaspoons chopped cilantro
Salt and white pepper to taste

✿

12 large live oysters in shells
2 cups coarsely shredded
    cabbage

If you're an oyster fan, your moment of indulgence has arrived. Serve these oysters raw or steamed, lavished with two delectable sauces. In the first, pungent salted black beans are nicely balanced with green onions and sesame oil. The second sauce is a mouth-watering version of garlic butter accented with shallots and cilantro.

Serves 4

1. Prepare the black bean sauce: Heat the cooking oil in a small frying pan over medium heat until hot. Add the garlic and ginger and cook for 10 seconds. Add the remaining ingredients and simmer until slightly thickened, about 3 minutes.

2. Prepare the garlic butter: Melt the butter in a small frying pan over medium heat. Add the garlic, shallot, and cilantro and cook until fragrant, 2 to 3 minutes. Season to taste with salt and pepper.

3. Open the oysters with an oyster knife, remove the flat top shells, and cut the oysters loose from the bottom shells. Top 6 of the oysters with black bean sauce and 6 with garlic butter. Serve on a bed of cabbage.

TIP: If you prefer the oysters cooked, steam them as follows: Make a nest of the cabbage in 2 heatproof glass pie dishes. Shuck the oysters and top with sauce as above; nestle half in each dish. Set one dish in a steamer or on a rack in a wok. Cover and steam over boiling water until the oysters begin to shrink and curl at the edge, 4 to 5 minutes. Repeat with the remaining oysters.

Another way to cook oysters is to barbecue them on the grill; there's no need to shuck them first. Put the unopened oysters directly on the grill, flat shell up. When the shells pop open, use an oyster knife to remove the top shells, add the sauce, and return the half-shell oysters to the grill just long enough to heat the sauce through.

Coconut Shrimp with Fruited Plum Sauce

Sauce
1 Asian pear or Golden
    Delicious apple, peeled,
    cored, and finely
    chopped
¼ cup plum sauce
1 tablespoon rice vinegar
1 teaspoon (packed) light
    brown sugar
1 teaspoon *each* minced fresh
    ginger and minced red
    ginger

❀

1 pound medium raw shrimp
½ teaspoon salt

Coconut Batter
1 cup all-purpose flour
1 teaspoon baking powder
1 teaspoon sugar
½ teaspoon curry powder
⅛ teaspoon cayenne
⅔ cup water
⅓ cup coconut milk

❀

1 cup unsweetened grated
    coconut
Cooking oil for deep-frying
Parsley sprigs

At most Chinese restaurants, crispy fried shrimp are everybody's favorite. If they're your favorite, you'll have to try this version. My crispy batter, laced with coconut shreds, gives extra texture and flavor to the sweet shrimp. Eat them plain, or dip them into the fruity sauce of plums and Asian pear; either way they're sure to be winners.

Makes about 36

1. Combine the sauce ingredients in a small serving bowl. Cover and chill until ready to serve.

2. Peel the shrimp, leaving the tail shells intact. Butterfly the shrimp by splitting them along the back and cutting almost all the way through. Remove the sand veins. Rinse the shrimp, pat dry with paper towels, and toss with the salt.

3. In a medium bowl, combine the flour, baking powder, sugar, curry powder, and cayenne. Add the water and coconut milk and stir until the batter is smooth. Holding a shrimp by the tail, dip it into the batter, then press in the grated coconut to coat all sides. Place the prepared shrimp in a single layer on a baking sheet. (May be prepared up to 4 hours ahead of time and refrigerated.)

4. Heat the oil to 340°F over medium-high heat. Add the shrimp a few at a time and deep-fry until golden brown, about 2 minutes. Lift out and drain on paper towels. Keep the shrimp warm in a 200°F oven while cooking the remaining shrimp.

5. Arrange the shrimp on a platter and garnish with parsley. Serve the dipping sauce alongside.

TIP: Unsweetened coconut is available in Asian markets and in health food stores. Do not substitute sweetened coconut; it contains sugar which may burn easily when deep-frying.

Spicy Teriyaki Wings

2 pounds whole chicken
    wings

Teriyaki Sauce

1 cup soy sauce
⅓ cup mirin (Japanese sweet
    rice wine)
⅓ cup (packed) light brown
    sugar
2 green onions, finely
    chopped
1 tablespoon minced ginger
¼ teaspoon crushed red
    pepper

✿

1 egg, lightly beaten
1 cup panko (Japanese-style
    bread crumbs) for dry-
    coating

These tender, juicy chicken wings with their sweet-spicy teriyaki marinade and crispy panko coating are so good you won't be able to stop asking for more. You won't have to feel guilty enjoying a few extra, because they are baked instead of deep-fried.

Makes about 20

1. Cut the chicken wings into sections; save the wing tips for stock (see Tip).

2. Heat the sauce ingredients in a small pan over low heat. Cook, stirring, until the sugar dissolves and the sauce thickens slightly, about 5 minutes. Let cool.

3. Pour half of the sauce into a medium bowl and add the wings. Let stand for 30 minutes. Reserve the remaining sauce.

4. Preheat the oven to 350°F. Lift the wings from their marinade and drain briefly. Dip in beaten egg, dredge in panko, and shake off the excess. Place the wings on a rack in a foil-lined baking pan. Bake until the wings are lightly browned and no longer pink, 30 to 35 minutes. Serve with the reserved teriyaki sauce as a dip.

TIP: Don't throw away the wing tips. Freeze them in a sealable plastic bag until you accumulate enough to flavor a simple chicken stock. Although they are small and look insignificant, they give a lot of gelatinous body to a stock. Simmer, uncovered, in enough water to cover the tips for about 1 hour. Strain and use as chicken broth.

Aromatic Rib Tea Soup

2 teaspoons cooking oil
2 large cloves garlic, lightly crushed
1½ pounds pork spareribs, excess fat removed, cut into 2-inch lengths
5 cups water
2 tablespoons dark soy sauce
1 tablespoon chopped green onion
2 teaspoons sugar
½ teaspoon salt
½ teaspoon white peppercorns
1 cinnamon stick
1 whole star anise

Chile Dip (optional)
2 tablespoons dark soy sauce
2 tablespoons regular soy sauce
1 jalapeño or serrano chile, thinly sliced
❀
Fried shallots (see Tip)

In the many homes and hawkers' stalls of Singapore, a favorite morning breakfast is not coffee and doughnuts, but pork rib tea soup and Chinese crullers. The locals call this tea soup because the cooking process creates an aromatic brew. Like tea, this soup warms your insides and helps prepare you for another day of hard work and excitement.

Serves 4

1. Heat a 5-quart pan over medium-high heat until hot. Add the oil, garlic, and ribs and cook until the meat is lightly browned on all sides, 4 to 5 minutes. Discard the pan drippings.

2. Add the water and bring to a boil. Simmer for 5 minutes; discard the scum that forms on top. Add the soy sauce, green onion, sugar, salt, peppercorns, cinnamon stick, and star anise. Cover and simmer for 45 minutes or until the ribs are very tender when pierced.

3. Combine the chile dip ingredients in a small bowl. To serve, place 2 or 3 ribs in each soup bowl, add a ladleful of broth, and sprinkle with a few fried shallots. Offer the chile dip alongside.

TIP: Fried shallots are as common as garlic and ginger in many Asian dishes. You can buy them already fried in Asian markets (sometimes labeled fried onions), but the best-tasting ones are made at home. To make your own, peel about a dozen shallots and slice them paper-thin. To assure even cooking, the slices must be of equal thickness. Heat oil to a depth of ½ inch in a small frying pan over medium heat. Add the shallots and cook, stirring, until they are crisp, dry, and golden brown, 4 to 6 minutes. Lift them out of the oil with a slotted spoon and drain on paper towels; when cool, place them in an airtight container and refrigerate. Strain and save the cooking oil; it has a nice shallot flavor and can be used in place of the cooking oil in most stir-fry recipes.

Goldfish Soup

Goldfish Mousse

¾ pound medium raw
   shrimp
1 tablespoon cornstarch
2 teaspoons dry sherry
1 teaspoon grated ginger
Pinch *each* of salt and white
   pepper
1 egg white, lightly beaten

❀

2 ounces thinly sliced
   Smithfield or Virginia
   ham
¼ cup frozen petite peas,
   thawed
4½ cups chicken broth
½ teaspoon sesame oil
Salt and white pepper to
   taste
6 slices regular tofu, drained
   and cut 1 inch wide, 1
   inch thick, and 2 inches
   long
6 snow peas, ends and
   strings removed
6 tiny carved carrot flowers,
   edible flowers, or chive
   blossoms (optional)

Everybody loves fish in our family—even goldfish. Fellow cooking teacher and good friend Gladys Lee makes this extraordinary soup with "fish" sculpted out of shrimp mousse. First she molds the fish between two Chinese porcelain spoons, then she decorates them with peas for eyes and slivers of ham for fins. It's a creative wonder that will delight all your friends and family.

The recipe makes enough mousse for 12 goldfish, but soup for only six. If you're going to make six fish, you might as well make an even dozen and freeze half for another time. Note that each fish needs its own spoon to steam in, plus one more for shaping—make sure you have enough spoons before you start!

Serves 6

1. Prepare the goldfish mousse: Peel and devein the shrimp and set the tail shells aside. In a food processor, coarsely chop the shrimp. Add the remaining mousse ingredients and process to make a smooth paste. Spray two porcelain Chinese soup spoons with nonstick spray. Mound 1½ tablespoons of the shrimp mixture in the bowl of one soup spoon. Turn the second spoon, bowl side down, onto the mousse to shape it further and smooth the edges. Lift off the top spoon and set the bottom spoon, filled with the mousse, aside. Repeat to form eleven more fish bodies.

2. Cut the sliced ham into 1- by ½-inch rectangles; notch the top of each rectangle so it looks like a fin. Decorate each spoonful of mousse so it looks like a fish, pressing two peas in the front for eyes, standing a slice of ham in the center for a fin, and tucking a reserved shrimp tail shell in the back for a tail.

3. Place the spoons on two heatproof plates. One at a time, place the plates on a rack, cover, and steam over boiling water until the mousse turns pink, 5 to 6 minutes. Carefully remove the goldfish from the spoons and place them on a plate.

4. Heat the chicken broth and sesame oil to simmering; add salt and pepper to taste. Place a piece of tofu in each individual soup bowl and top with a goldfish. Blanch the snow peas in the chicken broth for 1 minute; scoop them out with a slotted spoon and place one alongside each goldfish. Ladle the broth into the bowls. If you wish, garnish each soup with a carrot flower before serving.

TIPS: The goldfish can be made ahead of time and frozen. Gently remove the cooled cooked shrimp from the spoons, place in a shallow pan, and freeze. When frozen solid, pack them in a single layer in a rigid container, seal tightly, and return to the freezer. Before using, thaw in the refrigerator overnight. Reheat in the microwave or steam before serving in the soup.

To make a carrot flower, trim the end of a peeled carrot, making a short point. To make the petals, make a short diagonal cut with a sharp knife along the side of the carrot toward the point, but do not cut all the way through. Rotate the carrot and continue making 3 or 4 more petal cuts. To release the flower, twist the flower base and pull it off. Place the flower in cool water until ready to use. To make more flowers, trim the base to a short point and continue making petal cuts.

In Japan, chopsticks are the only eating utensil at the table. You might wonder "how do the Japanese eat soup with chopsticks?" They don't . . . they sip it right from the bowl. That's why Japanese soups are usually clear and simple with relatively few ingredients.

Hearty East-West Gazpacho

6 fresh shiitake mushrooms
1 avocado
2 cans (12 ounces each)
    vegetable juice cocktail
2 medium tomatoes, peeled,
    seeded, and diced
½ cucumber, peeled, seeded,
    and diced
½ cup diced red onion
½ cup diced jicama
2 tablespoons chopped
    cilantro
2 tablespoons chopped fresh
    Thai basil or regular
    basil
2 tablespoons chopped
    pickled ginger
2 tablespoons extra virgin
    olive oil
2 tablespoons sweet chili
    sauce
2 tablespoons rice vinegar
1 teaspoon minced garlic
1 teaspoon ground toasted
    Sichuan peppercorns (see
    page 28)
½ teaspoon salt
Cilantro sprigs

My good friend Bernice Fong and I share a passion for gardening. When I have a bumper crop in my vegetable garden, I always make Bernice's gazpacho. Served icy cold, it's a light and refreshing treat. There's no cooking required, so don't be put off by the long ingredient list. All you need to do is chop up all those garden-fresh vegetables, add the seasonings, and chill.

Serves 6 to 8

1. Cut off and discard the mushroom stems. Dice four of the mushroom caps and place them in a large bowl; set aside the remaining two caps for garnish. Halve the avocado, cut one half into ½-inch cubes, and add them to the mushrooms; cover the remaining half with plastic wrap and chill until ready to serve.

2. Combine the mushrooms and all the remaining ingredients except the cilantro; mix lightly. Cover and chill for at least 4 hours.

3. Just before serving, thinly slice the reserved mushrooms and avocado. Serve the soup in chilled bowls. Garnish each with a few mushroom slices, an avocado slice, and a sprig of cilantro.

TIP: Cooking instructions, East and West, frequently call for peeled, seeded tomatoes. To peel, first make a shallow cross incision with a sharp knife on the bottom of the tomato. Dip the tomato in boiling water for 30 seconds, then rinse in cold water to stop the cooking. Starting from the bottom, gently peel the skin away and remove the stem end. To seed, cut the tomato in half crosswise and gently squeeze each half to remove the seeds and juices. The peeled, seeded tomato is now ready to slice or dice.

Mixed Vegetable and Bean Soup

4 dried black mushrooms
½ cup frozen baby lima
    beans, thawed
8 cups chicken broth
4 slices ginger, lightly
    crushed
1 medium carrot, thinly
    sliced diagonally
1 can (about 8 ounces)
    garbanzo beans, drained
    and rinsed
1 can (about 8 ounces)
    kidney beans, drained
    and rinsed
2 cups Chinese (napa)
    cabbage, cut into 1-inch
    pieces
1 large tomato, peeled,
    seeded, and cut into 1-
    inch pieces
8 ounces soft tofu, drained
    and cut into ¾-inch
    cubes
2 tablespoons lemon juice
½ teaspoon sesame oil
1 green onion, thinly sliced

In a hurry? Don't worry. This fresh soup can be prepared quickly. Just empty your refrigerator of all its leftover vegetables and add a few handfuls of hearty lima, kidney, and garbanzo beans. Not only will the vegetables supply you with vitamins and minerals, the addition of beans will provide texture, color, and lots of complex carbohydrates and protein to keep you going. This soup has all the flavor of a slow-cooked soup without the long simmering usually required to obtain this depth of flavor.

Serves 6

1. Soak the mushrooms in warm water for 30 minutes; drain. Cut off the stems and quarter the caps. Cook the lima beans according to package directions.

2. In a large pot, bring the broth, mushrooms, and ginger to a boil over medium-high heat. Reduce the heat, cover, and simmer for 15 minutes. Add the carrot and beans and cook for 10 minutes. Add the cabbage, tomato, and tofu and cook for 5 minutes.

3. Season with the lemon juice and sesame oil. Sprinkle green onion over each serving.

TIP: Although this quick recipe calls for canned beans, dry beans may be substituted when time allows. Look for firm, clean whole dried beans of uniform size and color. To prepare dried beans for cooking, cover them with hot water and bring to a boil for a few minutes, remove from the heat, cover and let soak for 1 hour. Drain, rinse, and drain again. Return to the pot with fresh water to cover and bring to a gentle boil (avoid a vigorous boil, which will separate the skins from the beans). Cook 1 to 2 hours, depending on the tenderness desired.

Heavenly Artichoke Soup

4 medium artichokes
6 tablespoons rice vinegar or
  lemon juice
2 thin slices ginger, lightly
  crushed
2 cups chicken broth
1 teaspoon shredded ginger
2 teaspoons soy sauce
⅛ teaspoon white pepper
½ cup sliced asparagus
½ cup finely chopped onion
1 can (8 ounces) water
  chestnuts, rinsed,
  drained, and finely
  chopped
¼ cup finely chopped carrots
3 green onions, thinly sliced
3 tablespoons cornstarch
  dissolved in 3
  tablespoons water
1 egg white, lightly beaten

After you try this soup, you'll know why I call it "heavenly." The velvety smooth broth filled with a treasure trove of goods will warm your heart.

Serves 6

1. Rinse the artichokes. Prepare a bowl of acidulated water with half the vinegar or lemon juice and 3 to 4 cups water. Bend back the outer green leaves of the artichokes and snap them off at the base. Continue until the point where the leaves are half yellow and half green. Using a stainless steel knife to prevent discoloration, cut the stems level with the bases and trim away any remaining dark green from the bases. Cut off the tops where the green meets the yellow. Place each artichoke in the acidulated water as soon as you are done trimming it.

2. Combine 3 cups water, the remaining vinegar, and the sliced ginger in a large saucepan and bring it to a boil. Drain the trimmed artichokes and add them to the pan. Bring it back to a boil, reduce the heat to low, cover, and simmer until the artichokes are tender when pierced with the tip of a sharp knife, about 20 minutes. Drain and discard the liquid. Cut the artichokes in half and use a spoon to scrape out the fuzzy choke from each half. Slice the halves thinly.

3. Bring 4 cups of water and the broth, shredded ginger, soy sauce, and pepper to a boil. Add the asparagus, onion, water chestnuts, and carrots and simmer over medium-low heat until tender, about 5 minutes. Add the sliced artichokes and half of the green onions and cook 1 minute. Add the cornstarch solution and cook, stirring, until lightly thickened. Remove from the heat. While constantly stirring the soup, drizzle in the egg white to make egg flowers. Ladle into individual bowls and garnish with the remaining green onions.

Yin-Yang Chicken and Spinach Soup

Yin (Spinach Soup)

2 quarts water
1 teaspoon cooking oil
1 teaspoon salt
2 bunches spinach, stems
    removed
2 cups chicken broth
White pepper to taste
4 teaspoons cornstarch
    dissolved in 3
    tablespoons water
½ teaspoon sesame oil

Yang (Chicken Soup)

4 teaspoons cornstarch
2 tablespoons dry sherry
½ teaspoon sugar
¼ teaspoon white pepper
1½ cups chicken broth
½ pound boneless, skinless
    chicken, minced
1 egg white, lightly beaten

✿

½ teaspoon *each* white and
    black sesame seeds

The Chinese not only practice the yin-yang philosophy in their daily lives, they apply it to their cooking as well. In this soup, the spinach (yin) and chicken (yang) offer a contrast not only in color but in flavor; yet the soup is in perfect harmony. It's an interestingly colorful dish that pleases both eye and palate.

Serves 6

1. Prepare the spinach soup: Bring the water, cooking oil, and salt to a boil in a large pot. Add the spinach and cook for 2 minutes; drain. Wrap the spinach in a clean tea towel and twist the towel to extract all the liquid. Coarsely chop the spinach.

2. In the same pot, bring the chicken broth to a boil over medium-high heat. Add the chopped spinach and pepper to taste. Add the cornstarch solution and cook, stirring, until the soup boils and thickens. Add the sesame oil. Keep warm.

3. Prepare the chicken soup: Combine the cornstarch, sherry, sugar, pepper, and chicken broth in a 2-quart nonstick pan. Add the chicken and mix well (the mixture will look soupy); let stand for 15 minutes. Stirring constantly, bring to a boil over medium heat. Continue to stir and cook for 3 minutes or until thickened and creamy. Remove the pan from the heat; slowly drizzle in the egg white, stirring constantly, to form "egg flowers."

4. Pour the spinach soup and chicken soup into two separate large heatproof glass measuring cups or two heatproof pitchers with pouring spouts. Slowly and gently pour the soups simultaneously into the opposite sides of a large bowl to form the yin and yang sides. Sprinkle a small circle of white sesame seeds on top of the spinach soup and another of black sesame seeds on top of the chicken soup.

VARIATION: As an optional decoration, and to assist in maintaining the yin-yang pattern of the two soups, cut a firm tomato in half, lay each half cut side down, and slice thinly. Carefully overlap the half slices and arrange in an S-shaped wall across the center of the serving bowl (see photo).

Beijing Pork and Bean Thread Soup

4 ounces dried bean thread noodles
5 cups chicken broth
½ pound lean boneless pork, julienned
1 cup thinly sliced bok choy
1 small carrot, julienned
¼ cup julienned Sichuan preserved vegetable
2 tablespoons soy sauce
⅛ teaspoon white pepper
1 teaspoon sesame oil

Whenever I travel to the most northern parts of China, my friends offer me this hearty home-style soup. It is one of the most popular soups served in many households north of the Yangtze River. Transparent bean threads give a smooth, silky texture to this savory soup. Cooked bean threads are slippery and tricky to pick up in a spoon, but long noodles are thought to signify a long life, so cut at your own risk!

Serves 6 to 8

1. Soak the bean threads in warm water for 5 minutes; drain. If you wish, cut them into shorter lengths.

2. Bring the chicken broth to a boil in a large pot. Add the bean threads, pork, bok choy, carrot, preserved vegetable, soy sauce, and pepper. Simmer, uncovered, for 5 minutes. Stir in sesame oil and serve.

Seafood Seaweed Soup

Marinade
2 tablespoons dry sherry
2 teaspoons cornstarch
½ teaspoon salt
¼ teaspoon white pepper

✿

¼ pound raw shrimp, peeled, deveined, and cut into ½-inch cubes
¼ pound sea scallops, cut into ½-inch cubes
¼ pound white fish fillet, cut into ½-inch cubes
½ ounce Chinese-style dried seaweed
6 cups chicken broth
½ pound regular tofu, drained and cut into ½-inch cubes
1 green onion, thinly sliced
¼ cup sliced water chestnuts
1 tablespoon chopped cilantro
2 egg whites, lightly beaten
1 teaspoon sesame oil

The fresh taste and clean scent of the ocean is present in each spoonful of this soup. The flavor and delicate texture of the seafood combined with the rich color and flavor of seaweed give one the feeling of walking along the boardwalk of San Francisco's Fisherman's Wharf.

Serves 6 to 8

1. Combine the marinade ingredients in a medium bowl. Add the shrimp, scallops, and fish and stir to coat. Let stand for 30 minutes.

2. Reconstitute the seaweed in a bowl of cold water for 2 minutes; drain.

3. Bring the broth to a boil in a large pot. Add the seaweed and cook for 3 minutes over medium heat. Add the shrimp, scallops, and fish; cook for 3 minutes. Add the tofu, green onion, water chestnuts, and cilantro; cook for 2 minutes.

4. Remove the pot from the heat. Slowly drizzle in the egg whites, stirring constantly, to form "egg flowers." Stir in the sesame oil and serve.

TIP: Chinese dried seaweed, sold in round or square bundles in Asian markets, is coarser in texture than the more processed Japanese *nori*. When reconstituted, the purple, lacy dried leaves look like purple cellophane, and their mild aroma of the sea enhances most seafood dishes.

Snow Fungus and Potato Soup

2 pieces dried white fungus
  (snow fungus)
8 pieces dried black fungus
  (cloud ears)
½ pound boneless, skinless
  chicken
4 cups chicken broth
½ teaspoon sesame oil
½ teaspoon sugar
Pinch *each* of salt and white
  pepper
1 cup unseasoned mashed
  potato
1 tablespoon *each* chopped
  green onion and cilantro
1 tablespoon cornstarch
  dissolved in 1 tablespoon
  water
2 egg whites, lightly beaten

Mashed potato as a thickener is the totally unexpected ingredient in this velvety smooth, light, and healthful soup. The equally unexpected crunchiness comes from the snow fungus and cloud ear, which are common ingredients in many Chinese dishes. These fungi are believed to help heal the body and soul.

Serves 6

1. Soak the fungus in warm water for 30 minutes; drain and coarsely chop.

2. Place the chicken, broth, sesame oil, sugar, salt, pepper, and fungus in a large pot. Cover and bring to a boil, reduce the heat, and simmer until the chicken is no longer pink, about 15 minutes. Lift out the chicken, let it cool briefly, and cut it into ¼-inch cubes.

3. Return the chicken to the broth and add the mashed potato, green onion, and cilantro. Stir until the potato is blended into the broth; heat to simmering. Add the cornstarch solution and cook, stirring, until the soup boils and thickens.

4. Remove the pot from the heat; slowly drizzle in the egg whites, stirring constantly, to form "egg flowers."

Vegetables
and
Salads

Gourmet Garden Greens

Honey Vinaigrette

¼ cup rice vinegar
2 tablespoons honey
1 tablespoon sesame oil
¼ teaspoon crushed red
    pepper
¼ teaspoon salt
⅛ teaspoon white pepper
3 tablespoons walnut oil
1 tablespoon slivered lemon
    zest

✿

4- or 5-inch section lotus
    root *or* 1 cup julienned
    jicama
6 cups assorted salad greens,
    rinsed and crisped
¼ pound fresh enoki
    mushrooms, trimmed
½ cup Candied Walnuts (see
    page 179)
1 teaspoon slivered lemon
    zest

If you're tired of serving the same salad every night, try this version to spark up your menu. Lotus root adds a crisp texture and has great visual appeal. For the greens, pick a selection your family enjoys. Just be sure to serve them chilled and crisp. The vinaigrette is so good, it may become your own house dressing.

Serves 6

1. Prepare the dressing: In a medium bowl, whisk together the rice vinegar, honey, sesame oil, red pepper, salt, and pepper until smooth. Whisk in the walnut oil last to bind the dressing. Stir in the 1 tablespoon lemon zest.

2. Peel and thinly slice the lotus root; blanch it in boiling water for 2 minutes. Drain, rinse with cold water, and drain again.

3. Arrange the greens on six salad plates. Top each with an equal portion of the lotus root, mushrooms, and walnuts. Sprinkle a few slivers of lemon zest over each salad.

4. Pour the dressing over each salad and serve.

TIP: Compared to its ethereal pink blossom, the root of the lotus plant is an ugly duckling. It looks like a fat sausage, and sometimes comes to market still streaked with mud. But under the brown skin is creamy white flesh riddled with air passages that give a beautiful cross section when sliced.

Like apples, cut lotus root turns brown when exposed to air; for salads or whenever it will not be cooked immediately after cutting, drop the slices in a bowl of acidulated water to prevent browning.

Roast Duck and Greens with Soy Vinaigrette

Dressing

¼ cup roast duck juices, fat removed
2 tablespoons soy sauce
2 tablespoons rice vinegar
2 tablespoons chopped cilantro
1 tablespoon sugar
Pinch of salt

❀

½ of a Chinese roast duck
4 cups assorted salad greens, rinsed and crisped
1 green onion, cut into 1½-inch slivers
8 pitted prunes, each stuffed with a walnut half
¼ cup fried shallots (see Tip, page 47)

When I was a child in Guangzhou, China, I planned the route of my daily walk to take me on the streets where I could see the rows of mahogany-colored roast ducks hanging in the windows outside markets, restaurants, and barbecue stalls. The aroma and sight of their dripping juices made my mouth water; it still does today. That's why I created this salad, whose tastes take me back to my boyhood days while still satisfying my desire for Western-style crisp fresh greens.

Serves 4

1. Combine the dressing ingredients in a small bowl and whisk until smooth. Set aside.

2. Cut the duck breast from the carcass in one piece. Remove the skin and discard the fat. Cut the breast and skin crosswise into very thin slices. Remove the remaining meat from the carcass and cut it into shreds.

3. Set aside a few slices of the duck breast for garnish. Place the rest of the duck and the salad greens in a large bowl. Pour the dressing over and toss to coat evenly. Transfer to a serving platter. Garnish with the reserved duck breast slices, green onion, and prunes. Sprinkle shallots on top.

TIP: Most people think those bright red roast ducks hanging behind the front windows of Chinese restaurants are Peking ducks. Wrong! They are Cantonese-style roast ducks, which are seasoned, roasted, and served entirely differently from the Peking style. For this dish, buy a half duck, uncut, and be sure to ask for the duck juices. Keep the duck in a low oven until ready to carve, then bone and cut the meat into thin slices.

Five-Bean Salad with Artichokes

Dressing

3 tablespoons rice vinegar
3 tablespoons soy sauce
3 tablespoons cooking oil
2 tablespoons white fermented bean curd
1 tablespoon sesame oil
1½ tablespoons sugar
2 teaspoons grated ginger
¼ teaspoon white pepper

❀

½ pound frozen soybean pods or ½ cup frozen baby lima beans, thawed
¼ pound Chinese long beans or other green beans, cut diagonally into 1-inch pieces
1 can (about 1 pound) blackeyed peas or garbanzo beans, drained and rinsed
1 can (about 1 pound) kidney beans, drained and rinsed
1 cup soybean or mung bean sprouts
1 can (8 ounces) sliced water chestnuts, drained and rinsed
4 steamed artichoke hearts, diced
½ medium onion, sliced

The many different ways of using protein-packed, smooth-textured dried and canned beans continue to amaze me. This is a fun adaptation of the popular three-bean salad, with five kinds of beans (if you count the sprouts) tossed with tasty artichokes in an Asian-style dressing.

Serves 8 to 10

1. In a food processor or blender, process the dressing ingredients until smooth.

2. If using the soybeans, cook them in a pot of boiling salted water for 5 minutes. Drain, rinse with cold water, and drain again. Shell the soybeans. If using the lima beans, cook according to package directions. Blanch the long beans in a pot of boiling water for 1 minute. Drain, rinse with cold water, and drain again.

3. In a large bowl, combine the cooked beans and the remaining ingredients. Add the dressing and toss to coat evenly.

TIPS: Soybeans in the pod are sold frozen and can be found at most Asian grocery stores. Cook them briefly in boiling salt water and shell before eating. I like to eat them like peanuts, a bowl by my side as I read the newspaper or watch a game on the television.

Dried and canned beans are available at any supermarket. Some of the world's most flavorful and nutritious dry beans are harvested from the fertile soils of California. If you want to use dried kidney beans instead of canned, look for the light red variety rather than the darker variety which is used for canning.

Summer Somen Salad

Dressing

⅓ cup soy sauce
¼ cup rice vinegar
2 tablespoons cooking oil
2 tablespoons sesame oil
2 tablespoons toasted sesame
    seeds (see page 78)
1 tablespoon sugar
1 teaspoon salt

❀

8 ounces dried *somen* (fine
    wheat noodles)
2 cups shredded iceberg
    lettuce
½ English cucumber,
    julienned
3 ounces *kamaboko* (Japanese
    fish cake), thinly sliced
1 cup finely julienned
    Chinese barbecued pork
    or ham
3 green onions, thinly sliced
Golden egg threads (see Tip,
    page 156)
¼ cup shredded carrot
¼ cup chopped peanuts

The first pasta salad probably came from Southeast Asia rather than Italy. Cold noodle dishes have been common in Asian cuisines for centuries. In this delightful salad, delicately thin Japanese wheat noodles *(somen)* provide the foundation, and fish cake, barbecued pork, egg threads, and crunchy vegetables the frills.

Serves 4 to 6

1. Combine the dressing ingredients in a small bowl and whisk until the sugar dissolves. Set aside.

2. Cook the somen in a large pot of boiling water until tender but firm to the bite, about 3 minutes. Drain, rinse with cold water, and drain again.

3. Line a serving platter with the lettuce. Place the somen on top of the lettuce. Arrange the cucumber, kamaboko, barbecued pork, green onions, and egg threads over the somen. Sprinkle the carrot and peanuts on top.

4. Present the salad at the table, then pour the dressing over the somen and toss.

TIP: Perhaps you've seen bright pink or yellow logs of *kamaboko* in your Asian grocer's produce or deli section and wondered what it was. It's a traditional Japanese preparation of pureed fish and potato starch, tinted with food coloring, formed into shapes and steamed. Ready to eat with no cooking required, kamaboko has a slightly rubbery texture and absorbs other flavors well in soups and salads. Store in the refrigerator for up to a week.

Somen, also known as ramen, are Japanese noodles made from wheat flour, salt, and water. They are sold dried, in 8-ounce packages, or fresh. You may find them in different colors—green (made with tea powder), bright yellow (made with egg yolk), or pink (tinted with red perilla oil).

Citrus Salad with Raspberry Vinaigrette

Dressing

3 tablespoons raspberry vinegar

1 tablespoon honey

1 tablespoon cooking oil

2 teaspoons sesame oil

✿

2 oranges

2 grapefruits

3 cups assorted salad greens, rinsed and crisped

1 Asian pear or regular pear

¼ small red onion, thinly sliced

2 water chestnuts, thinly sliced

¼ cup chopped toasted walnuts

1 tablespoon slivered crystallized ginger

Of the many fresh fruits I was introduced to when I first came to North America, oranges and grapefruits are among my favorites. Here's your chance to try some of them in a fresh green salad served with a tangy raspberry dressing. Nowadays, assorted baby salad greens are available in bulk or in pre-packaged bags in the produce section of your local market. Use them to create a quick and elegant first course.

Serves 4

1. In a medium bowl, whisk together the vinegar and honey until smooth. Whisk in the oils until the dressing is creamy.

2. Cut the peel and all white membrane from the oranges and grapefruits. Cut between the segments, then lift out the segments.

3. Arrange the salad greens on a serving plate. Peel, core, and slice the pear. Arrange the pear slices, citrus segments, onion, and water chestnuts on top of the greens. Sprinkle the walnuts and ginger over the fruit. Drizzle the dressing over the top.

TIP: If you can't find premixed salad green combinations, mix your own using any combination of greens and endive that strikes your fancy. Butter and oak leaf lettuces have an interesting shape and soft texture that is especially pleasant with fruit. For color choose red leaf lettuce and radicchio. Other ideas would be curly endive for a slight bitterness; sorrel for tartness; spinach for deep green color and coarseness; and for a bite, watercress, Belgian endive, and arugula.

Artichokes with Cilantro-Lime Sauce

6 medium artichokes
6 thin slices ginger
3 tablespoons lemon juice

Cilantro-Lime Sauce
2 cups (lightly packed) cilantro leaves and stems
Zest of 1 lime, coarsely chopped
1 clove garlic, crushed and peeled
1½ teaspoons lime juice
½ teaspoon sesame oil
1½ teaspoons soy sauce
½ teaspoon sugar
4 teaspoons mayonnaise (regular or cholesterol free)

Before I came to the United States, I had never seen an artichoke, but the first sampling made me an instant fan. It's fun to pull off each leaf and scrape the tender base with your teeth. I call it a fun slow food which is meant to be savored slowly. Mayonnaise and melted butter are standard artichoke dips, but I like my artichokes with Asian seasonings such as those in this creamy sauce. Share this dish with that special someone.

Serves 6

1. Cut off the artichoke stems even with the base; slice off the top third of the leaves. Remove the coarse outer leaves and cut off the thorny tips of the remaining leaves with scissors. Stand the artichokes in a large deep pan. Add 2 inches of water and the ginger and lemon juice. Bring to a boil, cover, and simmer until the stem end is tender when pierced, 25 to 35 minutes. Drain.

2. Prepare the sauce: In a food processor, process the cilantro, lime zest, and garlic until finely chopped. Add the lime juice, sesame oil, soy sauce, and sugar; process to a smooth paste. Transfer to a bowl, add the mayonnaise, and whisk to blend evenly.

3. Serve the artichokes hot or cold on individual plates with the sauce alongside.

TIP: Artichokes are available year round, but their peak season is from March to May. High in vitamin C, magnesium, and fiber, they are nutritious and versatile. Choose plump, compact, heavy artichokes with a consistent green color. To store, drizzle with a few drops of water and store in a sealed plastic bag in the refrigerator.

To prevent raw artichokes from discoloring when cut, cook them in acidulated water—just add 3 tablespoons vinegar or lemon juice per quart of water.

Scallop Salad with Ginger-Lemon Dressing

Scallops, those succulent little morsels from the sea, are the main ingredient in this main-course salad. The light dressing, spiced with lemon and ginger, is the perfect compliment to the scallops. Bright strips of red pepper add a nice spot of color and a bit of sweetness.

Serves 4 to 6

Ginger-Lemon Dressing

¼ cup lemon juice
2 tablespoons sugar
1½ tablespoons minced
    ginger
1 teaspoon minced garlic
1 teaspoon salt
¼ teaspoon white pepper
3 tablespoons cooking oil
2 teaspoons sesame oil

❁

¾ pound bay scallops
1 teaspoon cornstarch
¼ teaspoon salt
2 tablespoons cooking oil
1 shallot, thinly sliced
1 small head butter lettuce,
    rinsed and crisped
1 small bunch watercress,
    tough stems removed,
    rinsed and crisped
4 ounces fresh enoki
    mushrooms, stem ends
    trimmed *or* fresh button
    mushrooms, sliced
½ red bell pepper, seeded
    and julienned

1. Combine the dressing ingredients in a small bowl and whisk until smooth. In another bowl, toss the scallops with the cornstarch and salt.

2. Heat a wok over high heat until hot. Add the oil and shallot and stir-fry for 10 seconds. Add the scallops and stir-fry until opaque, about 1 minute. Remove from the heat.

3. Arrange the lettuce and watercress on a large plate. Top with the mushrooms and bell pepper. Arrange the warm scallops over the top. Pour the dressing over the salad and serve.

Warm Beef Salad

Marinade
½ small onion, finely
    chopped
2 tablespoons fish sauce
1 tablespoon cooking oil
1 tablespoon minced shallots
2 teaspoons minced garlic
1 teaspoon sugar
¼ teaspoon black pepper
⅛ teaspoon salt

❀

¾ pound flank steak

Dressing
2 tablespoons rice vinegar
2 tablespoons cooking oil
1 tablespoon sesame oil
¼ teaspoon black pepper

❀

4 cups assorted salad greens,
    rinsed and crisped
½ small red onion, thinly
    sliced tip to tip
½ cup finely julienned
    English cucumber
1 small carrot, finely
    julienned
½ cup cilantro leaves
¼ cup fresh basil, julienned

I've adapted this unusual entree salad from a Vietnamese classic. You could make it with leftover steak but, to my way of thinking, it tastes best when the meat is grilled or barbecued at the last minute and tossed with the salad while it is still warm and juicy.

Serves 4

1. Combine the marinade ingredients in a shallow pan. Add the meat and turn to coat. Let stand for 30 minutes.

2. In a small bowl, whisk the dressing ingredients together and set aside. Place the salad greens in a wide, shallow bowl. Arrange the onion, cucumber, carrot, cilantro, and basil over the greens.

3. Place the beef on a greased grill over a solid bed of hot glowing coals. Cook until browned on the outside but still pink within, 4 to 5 minutes on each side. Slice the meat crosswise into thin slices; arrange over the salad. Pour the dressing over the salad and toss.

Wild Rice Salad with Orange-Walnut Vinaigrette

1½ cups wild rice, rinsed
   and drained
3 cups chicken broth

Dressing
⅓ cup orange juice
3 tablespoons soy sauce
2 teaspoons sesame oil
1 teaspoon sugar
¼ teaspoon salt
1 teaspoon ground toasted
   Sichuan peppercorns
2 tablespoons walnut oil

❀

½ cup diced celery
½ cup sliced button
   mushrooms
½ cup sliced fresh shittake
   mushrooms
2 green onions, thinly sliced
2 tablespoons chopped
   cilantro
½ cup chopped pitted prunes
½ cup walnuts, coarsely
   chopped
Zest of 1 orange

Wild rice isn't really a rice, but the seeds of another aquatic grass native to Minnesota. Today, these aromatic little brown kernels are also harvested in the sun-drenched Sacramento Valley of California. Their special nutty flavor and chewy texture will make you "wild" for more of this delicious salad.

Serves 4 to 6

1. Combine the wild rice and chicken broth in a medium saucepan. Bring to a boil, cover, reduce the heat, and simmer until tender, 45 to 50 minutes. Drain off any liquid remaining in the pan.

2. While the rice cooks, combine all the dressing ingredients except the walnut oil in a small bowl and whisk until smooth. Whisk in the walnut oil last to bind the dressing.

3. Transfer the rice to a large bowl and let it cool. Add the celery, mushrooms, green onions, and cilantro. Add the dressing, prunes, and walnuts and stir to coat evenly. Sprinkle orange zest on top.

TIP: Depending on the variety, wild rice can take 35 to 50 minutes to cook and triples or quadruples in volume. The grains should be cooked until they are tender and open, showing their coffee-colored interior, but not so long that they become mushy. Tightly covered and stored in a cool dry place or in the freezer, uncooked wild rice keeps indefinitely.

Chinese Vegetable Bouquet

14 medium dried black
  mushrooms
½ cup vegetable broth
  (canned or homemade)
2 tablespoons dry sherry
1 teaspoon minced ginger
1 teaspoon minced garlic
1 teaspoon salt
⅛ teaspoon white pepper
½ teaspoon cooking oil
6 baby Shanghai bok choy,
  cut in half lengthwise
1 medium tomato, peeled,
  cut into 6 wedges, seeds
  removed
2 teaspoons cornstarch
  dissolved in 1 tablespoon
  water

At most formal Chinese banquets or lavish restaurant dinners, you'll be served this traditional Northern vegetable dish of beautiful vegetables artfully arranged in the shape of a big flowering bouquet. Use any combination of vegetables that will give you the contrasts of vivid color and varying texture.

Serves 6

1. Soak the mushrooms in warm water for 30 minutes; drain, reserving ½ cup of the soaking liquid in a medium pan. Discard the mushroom stems and leave the caps whole. To the mushroom soaking liquid add the vegetable broth, sherry, ginger, garlic, ½ teaspoon of the salt, and pepper; bring to a boil. Add the mushrooms, cover, and simmer for 15 minutes. Lift the mushrooms out with a slotted spoon and set aside. Reserve the mushroom broth.

2. Bring a large pot of water to a boil. Add the oil, remaining salt, and bok choy. Cook until the bok choy is crisp-tender, 3 to 4 minutes. Lift out the bok choy, place it in a colander, rinse with cold water, and drain again. In the same water, blanch the tomato pieces for 30 seconds. Drain, rinse with cold water, and drain again.

3. Arrange the vegetables on a platter so they form a bouquet. Group the bok choy, cut side down, at one end for the stems. Place the mushrooms in the middle to form a bow, and arrange the tomato "petals" at the top to form the bouquet (see photo).

4. Heat the reserved mushroom broth to boiling over medium-high heat. Add the cornstarch solution and cook, stirring, until the sauce boils and thickens slightly. Pour the sauce over the vegetables to give them a shiny glaze.

TIP: Baby Shanghai bok choy is shaped like the familiar

white-ribbed bok choy, but is smaller, with greenish stems and light green leaves. It is sold in bunches of 3 or 4 and is available most of the year. You can also use baby white-stemmed bok choy, but the color will be different.

Thai Cabbage Salad

Dressing
2 tablespoons fish sauce
2 tablespoons lime juice
1 tablespoon sugar
2 tablespoons walnut oil
1 tablespoon slivered lime
    zest

Slaw
3 cups shredded regular
    cabbage or Chinese
    (napa) cabbage
1 small red onion, thinly
    sliced
1 medium carrot, shredded
2 tablespoons chopped
    cilantro
2 tablespoons chopped fresh
    mint

❀

Cooking oil for deep-frying
12 wonton skins, cut into
    ¼-inch-wide strips

Here's a spunky variation on everyday coleslaw. Cilantro, mint, and a mild sweet-sour dressing give this salad a refreshing bite that goes especially well with chili-spiked meat and poultry in any menu. If you wish to make this a heartier salad, toss in a handful of cooked baby shrimp.

Serves 4 to 6

1. Combine the dressing ingredients in a small bowl and whisk until smooth. Combine the slaw ingredients in a large bowl, cover, and refrigerate until ready to serve.

2. Heat the oil over medium heat to 360°F. Deep-fry the wonton strips until golden brown, about 15 seconds. Lift them out with a skimmer and drain on paper towels.

3. Pour the dressing over the slaw and toss. Serve the salad in a wide shallow bowl surrounded with the wonton strips.

Chilled Tofu Salad

1 pound regular or soft tofu, drained and cut into 1½-inch squares ½ inch thick

Dressing
3 tablespoons soy sauce
1 teaspoon sesame oil
1 teaspoon chili oil
1 teaspoon grated ginger
½ teaspoon sugar

Garnishes
1 tablespoon cooking oil
2 tablespoons dried shrimp
2 tablespoons chopped Sichuan preserved vegetable
2 tablespoons fried shallots (see page 47)
2 tablespoons chopped peanuts
1 green onion, chopped

You could serve this in individual bowls, but for looks I like to stack the tofu pyramid style in a shallow bowl, surrounded with the flavorful garnishes, and with the dressing puddled in the middle. To eat, just drizzle a cube of creamy tofu with the dressing, sprinkle with your favorite garnishes, and enjoy. Simple and delectably satisfying!

Serves 6

1. Arrange the tofu in a flat shallow bowl or on a rimmed plate, leaving a 3-inch circle open in the center. Cover and chill until ready to serve. Combine the dressing ingredients in a small bowl and whisk until smooth.

2. Heat the oil in a small frying pan over medium heat until hot. Add the shrimp and cook for 2 minutes. Let stand until cool, then coarsely chop.

3. Individually mound the shrimp and the other garnishes around the tofu. Pour the dressing in the center of the bowl. To eat, place the tofu and garnishes into small individual serving bowls, then spoon the dressing over.

TIP: Dried shrimp are usually soaked before using to soften them, but for this dish I like to stir-fry them straight from the bag.

In ancient China, people's fortunes were read by the way they held their chopsticks. If you used two fingers, it meant you'd have a carefree life. Four fingers meant good fortune. Five fingers meant you were destined for greatness. Of course, 10 fingers just meant you didn't know how to use the darn things!

Chicken Salad with Honey-Mustard Dressing

Dressing
½ cup mayonnaise
1½ tablespoons Chinese
    mustard
1½ tablespoons honey
1½ tablespoons soy sauce
1 tablespoon sesame oil
2 teaspoons chili oil

❀

¼ pound snow peas, ends
    and strings removed
1 cup julienned jicama
1 red bell pepper, seeded and
    julienned
2 cups shredded cooked
    chicken
1 small head red or green
    leaf lettuce, rinsed and
    crisped
1 cup toasted walnuts

Chinese chicken salad is such a popular dish I think it's smart to have two or even three variations up your sleeve. This one reflects the thinking of the new generation of young Chinese cooks who are beginning to incorporate Western ingredients into some of their dishes. Try this modern approach to an old favorite.

Serves 4 to 6

1. In a medium bowl, whisk together the dressing ingredients until smooth.

2. Blanch the snow peas in boiling water for 1 minute or until crisp-tender. Drain, rinse with cold water, and drain again. Place in a large bowl and add the jicama, bell pepper, and chicken. Cover and refrigerate until ready to serve.

3. Line a serving dish with lettuce. Spoon the dressing over the chicken mixture, stir to coat evenly, and place on top of the greens. Sprinkle with the toasted walnuts.

 In ancient China, people believed that a childless couple could change their luck by stealing a pair of chopsticks from a couple with a lot of children. For twins, you had to steal two pairs. And if you wanted a really big family, you had to steal two woks, a spatula, and a set of bamboo steamers!

Triple Mushroom Roundup

¼ cup dried black fungus (cloud ears)
½ pound fresh shiitake or oyster mushrooms
½ pound fresh white or brown button mushrooms
2 bunches (about 1½ pounds) spinach, stems removed, rinsed, and drained
1 tablespoon cooking oil
1 tablespoon minced shallot
2 teaspoons minced garlic
⅔ cup chicken broth
1 teaspoon sesame oil
½ teaspoon salt
½ teaspoon sugar
¼ teaspoon white pepper
1½ teaspoons cornstarch dissolved in 1 tablespoon water

When I was growing up, my mom kept telling me, "eat your mushrooms," and I did. Now I am telling everybody who watches the Yan Can Cook show, "eat your mushrooms." They are not only delicious and versatile, but they are also good for your body.

Serves 4 to 6

1. Soak the cloud ears in warm water for 30 minutes; drain. Trim the ends of the shiitake or oyster mushroom stems; leave these mushrooms whole. Thinly slice the button mushrooms.

2. Blanch the spinach in a large pot of boiling water for 2 minutes or until wilted; drain. Spread the spinach on a serving platter; cover loosely to keep warm.

3. Heat a wok over medium-high heat until hot. Add the cooking oil, shallot, and garlic and stir-fry for 10 seconds. Add the cloud ears and chicken broth. Cover and cook for 3 minutes. Add the mushrooms, sesame oil, salt, sugar, and pepper; stir until the mushrooms are tender, about 2 minutes. Add the cornstarch solution and cook, stirring, until the sauce boils and thickens. Pour over the spinach and serve.

TIPS: Some studies have indicated a possibility that consumption of black fungus (cloud ears and tree ears) slows down the clotting of blood and lowers the cholesterol level.

To clean mushrooms, wipe them with a damp cloth or lightly scrub with a mushroom brush. If you decide to wash the mushrooms, wait until just before you are ready to use them, and rinse them quickly in cool water. Do not keep them under water too long, as they quickly absorb a lot of water which they release when cooking.

Snappy Stir-Fry

½ cup julienned pickled
　　radish strips
¼ cup dried black fungus
　　(cloud ears)
8 dried black mushrooms

Sauce
¼ cup chicken broth
3 tablespoons soy sauce
1½ teaspoons sugar
1 teaspoon sesame oil

✿

1 tablespoon cooking oil
4 whole dried chile peppers
2 thin slices ginger, julienned
1 small onion, thinly sliced
1 cup fresh button
　　mushrooms, sliced
¼ pound ham or Chinese
　　barbecued pork, thinly
　　sliced
¼ cup chicken broth
½ pound sugar snap peas,
　　ends removed
1 teaspoon cornstarch
　　dissolved in 2 teaspoons
　　water

This recipe contains many of my favorite Chinese vegetables. It is easy to prepare and can be put together while the other parts of your meal are cooking. You'll find the traditional Chinese pickled radish strips are a tasty ingredient that will mystify your family and friends. Even if you can't find the pickled radish for this dish, your creation will still be pretty snappy!

Serves 4 to 6

1. Soak the pickled radish in warm water for 1 hour; drain. Soak the cloud ears and black mushrooms in warm water for 30 minutes; drain. Leave the cloud ears whole. Discard the mushroom stems and thinly slice the caps. Combine the sauce ingredients in a small bowl.

2. Heat a wok over high heat until hot. Add the oil, chiles, and ginger and stir-fry for 30 seconds. Add the radish strips, cloud ears, black mushrooms, and onion; stir-fry for 1 minute. Add the button mushrooms, ham, and chicken broth, cover, and cook for 2 minutes. Add the sugar snap peas, cover, and cook until the peas are crisp-tender, about 1 minute. Add the sauce and cornstarch solution and cook, stirring, until the sauce boils and thickens.

76

Long Beans with Pressed Bean Curd

Chinese long beans look like green ropes of licorice often reaching lengths of three feet. That's why you may find this green wonder under the name "yard long beans." Although similar in taste to regular green beans, long beans are thinner and crunchier. Not every market will have these beans, but you can always grow your own. You'll enjoy long beans with the bite of the curry-accented seasonings and the high protein content of the pressed curd.

Serves 4 to 6

Sauce
⅓ cup chicken broth
2 tablespoons dry sherry
2 tablespoons rice vinegar
1 tablespoon mushroom soy sauce
1 tablespoon curry powder *or* 2 tablespoons bottled curry paste
2 teaspoons sugar
Pinch of ground toasted Sichuan peppercorns
Pinch of crushed red pepper

❀

6 wood ears (black fungus)
½ pound Chinese long beans or regular green beans
1 tablespoon cooking oil
1 teaspoon minced garlic
1 teaspoon minced ginger
1 small carrot, julienned
½ medium red onion, cut crosswise into thin strips
4 ounces pressed bean curd, julienned
1½ teaspoons cornstarch dissolved in 1 tablespoon water
1 tablespoon toasted sesame seeds

1. Combine the sauce ingredients in a small bowl; set aside.

2. Soak the wood ears in warm water for 30 minutes; drain. Cut off the hard knobs in the centers of the wood ears; cut the wood ears into ¼-inch julienne strips.

3. Remove the ends of the beans; cut the beans diagonally into 1½-inch lengths. Blanch them in boiling water for 30 seconds; drain.

4. Heat a wok over high heat until hot. Add the cooking oil, garlic, and ginger and stir-fry for 10 seconds. Add the wood ears, beans, carrot, onion, and bean curd. Stir-fry for 30 seconds. Add the sauce, cover, and cook until the beans are crisp-tender, about 3 minutes. Add the cornstarch solution and cook, stirring, until the sauce boils and thickens. Place in a serving bowl and sprinkle with the sesame seeds.

TIPS: Mushroom soy sauce is a dark soy sauce (see page 29) flavored with straw mushrooms and a bit of sugar. If you can't find it, use dark soy sauce.

To toast sesame seeds, place them in a small ungreased frying pan over medium heat and shake or stir until lightly golden brown and fragrant. Store raw or toasted seeds airtight in the refrigerator or freezer to prevent rancidity.

Broccoli and Cauliflower Stir-Fry

2 teaspoons cooking oil
2 teaspoons minced garlic
1 ½ cups broccoli florets
1 ½ cups cauliflower florets
1 can (8 ounces) straw
    mushrooms, drained
½ cup chicken broth
2 tablespoons oyster sauce
2 teaspoons sesame oil
¼ teaspoon white pepper
1 teaspoon cornstarch
    dissolved in 2 teaspoons
    water

When I was growing up in China, I never heard the phrase "an apple a day keeps the doctor away." Where I come from, we got our vitamins from eating fresh vegetables. This supermarket stir-fry, so named because broccoli and cauliflower are found in every market's produce section, is high in vitamins A and C. The yin-yang color and similar texture make this a great vegetable side dish for any meal.

Serves 4 to 6

1. Heat a wok over high heat until hot. Add the cooking oil and garlic and stir-fry for 10 seconds. Add the broccoli, cauliflower, and mushrooms and stir-fry for 30 seconds. Add the chicken broth, cover, and cook until the vegetables are crisp-tender, about 3 minutes.

2. Add the oyster sauce, sesame oil, and pepper and cook for 1 minute. Add the cornstarch solution and cook, stirring, until the sauce boils and thickens.

TIP: To eliminate any undesirable "canned" taste from straw mushrooms, drain them, dip them in boiling water for 1 minute, and drain before using. I do the same for canned bamboo shoots, water chestnuts, and baby corn.

 Never give newlyweds disposable chopsticks as a wedding present — unless you want the marriage to end in divorce! Disposable chopsticks are meant to be split apart and thrown away, so keep them off your wedding gift list!

Tianjin Cabbage Rolls

10 dried black mushrooms

Sauce

2 tablespoons rice vinegar
1 teaspoon sugar
1 teaspoon sesame oil
¼ teaspoon Chinese five-
    spice
½ teaspoon salt
⅛ teaspoon white pepper

✿

1 tablespoon cooking oil
1 teaspoon *each* minced garlic
    and ginger
4 ounces pressed bean curd,
    julienned
2 ounces Sichuan preserved
    vegetable, julienned
1 small carrot, julienned
¼ pound soybean or mung
    bean sprouts
1 teaspoon cornstarch
    dissolved in 2 teaspoons
    water
2 tablespoons chopped
    cilantro or 2 green
    onions, chopped
8 large Chinese (napa)
    cabbage leaves

The beauty of these sushi-like rolls is that they are pretty to look at and delightful to eat. They are also quite easy to prepare and can be made ahead of time and placed on a serving platter ready for your guests when they arrive. You can serve them at room temperature or slightly chilled.

Makes 16 rolls

1. Soak the mushrooms in warm water for 30 minutes; drain. Discard the stems and thinly slice the caps. Combine the sauce ingredients in a small bowl.

2. Heat a wok over medium-high heat until hot. Add the oil, garlic, and ginger and stir-fry for 10 seconds. Add the mushrooms, bean curd, preserved vegetable, carrot, bean sprouts, and sauce. Stir-fry for 3 minutes. Add the cornstarch solution and cook, stirring, until the sauce boils and thickens. Stir in the cilantro, transfer the mixture to a bowl, and let cool.

3. Drop the cabbage leaves in a large pot of simmering water and cook just until limp, 2 to 3 minutes. Drain, rinse with cold water, and drain again. Pat the leaves dry between paper towels. Cut the leaves to make rectangles about 3½ by 7 inches; discard the heavy stem ends. As needed, use a knife to shave any remaining thick white ribs to make the leaves easier to roll.

4. Place each leaf on a work surface with the stem end facing you. Spread ¼ cup of the filling in a band across the bottom of the leaf. Roll the leaf tightly to enclose the filling and make a compact roll. Repeat to make 8 rolls. If made ahead, cover and chill until ready to serve.

5. To serve, trim the ends of each roll and cut the rolls in half. Stand the rolls on a serving plate so the colorful filling shows.

Pork-Filled
Bitter
and
Fuzzy Melons

Pork Filling

6 dried black mushrooms
½ pound lean pork, minced
    or ground
2 water chestnuts, finely
    chopped
2 green onions, minced
1 tablespoon chopped
    Sichuan preserved
    vegetable
1 teaspoon sesame oil
¼ teaspoon *each* salt and
    black pepper
2 teaspoons cornstarch
1 egg, lightly beaten

❀

1 cucumber-shaped fuzzy
    melon
2 bitter melons
About ½ cup cornstarch for
    dusting
2 tablespoons cooking oil
¾ cup chicken broth
2 tablespoons black bean
    sauce (see Tips) or oyster
    sauce
1 teaspoon cornstarch
    dissolved in 2 teaspoons
    water

The bite of bitter melon is not everyone's cup of tea, but the Chinese relish the sharp quinine-like taste just as the Italians enjoy endive, escarole, and other bitter greens. A favorite way to use this vegetable is to remove the seeds, cut it into rings, and cook them with a savory meat filling. For a milder tasting contrast, try stuffing fuzzy melon, also known as fuzzy squash. Use the long thin variety that looks like a cucumber, not the round squat variety.

Serves 6 to 8

1. Soak the mushrooms in warm water for 30 minutes; drain. Discard the stems and mince the caps. In a medium bowl, combine the mushrooms, pork, water chestnuts, green onions, preserved vegetable, sesame oil, salt, pepper, cornstarch, and egg; mix well.

2. Peel the fuzzy melon or scrape off the fuzz with a knife. Cut the bitter melons and fuzzy melon into 1-inch-thick rounds. Remove the seed-filled cores with a teaspoon or melon baller. Lightly dust the inner surfaces with the cornstarch and tightly pack each core with pork filling. Place the rounds on a baking sheet dusted with cornstarch.

3. Heat the oil in a wide frying pan over medium-high heat until hot. Place the stuffed rounds in the pan and cook until lightly browned, about 1 minute on each side. Add the chicken broth. Reduce the heat to medium-low, cover, and simmer until the melons are tender and the pork filling is no longer pink, about 10 minutes. Lift the rounds out with a slotted spatula and place on a platter. Add the black bean sauce to the pan juices. Add the cornstarch solution and cook, stirring, until the sauce boils and thickens. Spoon the sauce over the melons.

TIPS: I always have a jar of black bean sauce in my refrigerator ready to use. To make your own, rinse and drain ¼ cup salted black beans; lightly crush them in a small bowl. Heat a wok over medium heat until hot and add 2 tablespoons cooking oil and 1 tablespoon minced garlic. Cook until fragrant, then add the black beans, 3 tablespoons dry sherry, 2 tablespoons dark soy sauce, 1 tablespoon brown sugar, and 2 teaspoons sesame oil. Cook, stirring, until fragrant, 2 to 3 minutes. Store in an airtight container and refrigerate. Use 2 to 3 tablespoons of the sauce in your favorite steamed, stir-fried, or braised dish. If you don't have time to make your own, ready-made black bean sauces are sold in any Asian market.

If you wish to tame the taste of bitter melon, parboil the rounds in salted water for 2 minutes, drain, and stuff as directed above. The pungency of the black bean sauce is a great complement to the bitter taste of the melon.

Peanutty Corn on the Cob

Marinade

¼ cup soy sauce
¼ cup dry sherry, apple juice, or white grape juice
¼ cup smooth peanut butter
3 tablespoons honey

✿

6 ears fresh corn, husks removed, each cut into three pieces
18 pieces aluminum foil, 6 by 8 inches

When I travel around the country to do cooking demonstrations, about 30 percent of the audience is made up of young children. I know kids love cooking and here's a great way to get them involved. Let them shuck the corn, season it with the peanut butter sauce, and wrap it in foil for grilling. Older kids can help tend the barbecue. You'll be amazed how well your kids can cook.

Serves 6

1. Combine the marinade ingredients in a large bowl. Add the corn and stir to coat. Let stand for 30 minutes.

2. Center a piece of corn on one piece of foil. Drizzle 1 teaspoon of the marinade over the corn. Bring the long sides of the foil together; fold to seal. Double the folded ends. Squeeze the foil tightly around the corn to make a snug package. Wrap the remaining corn.

3. Place the corn on an oiled grill over a solid bed of glowing coals. Grill for 15 minutes, turning occasionally.

Buddha's Spaghetti

1 spaghetti squash, 3 to 4 pounds
1 tablespoon cooking oil
2 teaspoons minced ginger
½ teaspoon salt
¼ teaspoon crushed red pepper
1 medium carrot, finely julienned
2 green onions (green part only), cut into 2-inch lengths and shredded
2 tablespoons mirin (Japanese sweet rice wine)
2 teaspoons sugar
1 teaspoon toasted sesame seeds

Spaghetti squash has been around for a long time but it didn't make headlines until a few years ago when calorie counters discovered it was a good stand-in for pasta. In this dish, I've combined it with carrots to make a simple side dish which you can serve warm as a vegetable or at room temperature as a salad. Like pasta, spaghetti squash loses its desirable texture if overcooked. Bake just until the shell gives to light pressure before separating the flesh into strands.

Serves 6

1. Preheat the oven to 350°F. Pierce the unpeeled squash with a fork in several places to allow steam to escape. Place the whole squash in a rimmed baking pan. Bake, uncovered, for 45 minutes; turn the squash over and continue to bake until it feels slightly soft when squeezed, another 15 to 30 minutes.

2. Cut the squash in half lengthwise and discard the seeds. With a fork, scoop the spaghetti-like strands of flesh into a bowl. Measure 3 cups of squash; reserve the remaining squash for another meal.

3. Heat a wok over medium-high heat until hot. Add the oil, ginger, salt, red pepper, and carrot; cook, stirring, until the carrot is crisp-tender, about 1 minute. Add the squash, green onion tops, mirin, and sugar; toss and cook until the vegetables are glazed and most of the liquid has evaporated, about 1 minute. The squash should remain crunchy in texture.

3. Transfer to a serving bowl and sprinkle with the sesame seeds. Serve warm or at room temperature.

Fish
and
Shellfish

Catfish with Black Vinegar Sauce

1 to 1½ pounds catfish
    fillets, about ½ inch
    thick
½ teaspoon salt
½ teaspoon white pepper

Sauce
1 teaspoon cooking oil
1 teaspoon minced ginger
1 teaspoon minced garlic
¼ cup Chinese dark rice
    vinegar or balsamic
    vinegar
2 tablespoons dry sherry or
    Chinese rice wine
1 tablespoon sugar
1 tablespoon soy sauce
2 tablespoons sweet chili
    sauce
1 teaspoon cornstarch
    dissolved in 2 teaspoons
    water

❀

1 egg, lightly beaten
About ¼ cup cornstarch for
    dry-coating
2 teaspoons cooking oil
1 green onion, cut into 1½-
    inch lengths and slivered

The rich color and full-bodied flavor of dark rice vinegar brings this catfish to life. The catfish, with relatively few bones and a subtle sweet taste, has been a Chinese favorite for centuries. Now restaurant chefs in America have discovered how wonderful catfish is and are preparing it in a great many dishes.

Serves 4

1. Sprinkle the fish with the salt and pepper. Let stand for 15 minutes.

2. Prepare the sauce: Heat a small pot over medium-high heat until hot. Add the oil, ginger, and garlic and cook for 10 seconds. Add the remaining sauce ingredients except the cornstarch solution and bring to a boil. Add the cornstarch solution and cook, stirring, until the sauce boils and thickens. Keep warm.

3. Dip the fish in the egg; drain briefly, then dust with the cornstarch. Heat the remaining oil in a wide non-stick frying pan over medium-high heat until hot. Place the fish in the pan and cook until golden brown and opaque in the center, about 3 minutes on each side. Transfer the fish to a serving platter. Pour the sauce over the fish and sprinkle with the green onion.

Tea-Smoked Salmon Fillet

Marinade

3 tablespoons regular soy
    sauce
1 tablespoon dark soy sauce
1 tablespoon dry sherry
2 teaspoons minced garlic
2 teaspoons minced ginger
Pinch of Chinese five-spice

❀

1 pound salmon fillets with
    skin, about ½ inch thick

Tea Mixture

½ cup (packed) brown sugar
½ cup uncooked rice
¼ cup black or oolong tea
    leaves
4 whole star anise
8 thin slices ginger

Once in a while, I even amaze myself. Believe me, I've never tasted salmon this good. The sweet, rich flavors of dark soy sauce and spices permeate the salmon fillet, but the real secret rests in the burning tea mixture, which gives the salmon its delicate, profoundly sweet, smoky flavor. When I entertain, I make this ahead of time and serve it hot or chilled.

Serves 4

1. Combine the marinade ingredients in a medium bowl. Add the salmon fillets and turn them once to coat. Cover and refrigerate for 2 hours.

2. Preheat the oven to 400°F. Set the oven rack in its lowest position (or, if you have a gas oven, remove the rack so a pan will sit directly on the oven floor). Line the bottom of a deep roasting pan with heavy-duty foil. Combine the tea mixture ingredients on the foil; mix well and spread in an even layer. Place 2 empty 2-inch-high cans (such as water chestnut cans) at each end of the pan and position a wire rack large enough to hold the salmon on the cans.

3. Place the fish on the rack. Cover the entire pan with a large sheet of foil, making a tent; seal the edges. Place the pan in the oven and bake until the center of the fish is opaque, about 10 minutes.

TIP: This is the tea mixture used for the famous classic Chinese dish, Tea Smoked Duck.

 In Japan, the polite—and sanitary—way to serve yourself from a communal bowl is by reversing your chopsticks and using the opposite end. This method has recently become popular in China, too.

Mushroom-Filled Salmon "Sandwiches"

Filling
4 dried black mushrooms
¼ cup finely julienned carrot
¼ cup fresh enoki
    mushrooms
¼ cup julienned celery
4 cilantro sprigs

Sauce
⅓ cup chicken broth
⅓ cup Shao Hsing wine or
    dry sherry
1½ tablespoons fish sauce
1 tablespoon minced shallots
1 stalk lemongrass, bottom 6
    inches, lightly crushed

✿

1 pound center cut salmon
    fillet, about 6 by 6
    inches by 1 inch thick,
    skinned
¼ teaspoon salt
¼ teaspoon black pepper
½ teaspoon sesame oil
2 tablespoons cooking oil
1 teaspoon cornstarch
    dissolved in 2 teaspoons
    water
Lemon wedges

Looking for a creative way to use fresh flavorful salmon? Split it into two layers, with finely julienned vegetables layered in between. Once the "sandwich" is assembled, it is browned and laced with a delectable lemongrass-accented wine sauce.

Serves 4

1. Soak the black mushrooms in warm water for 30 minutes; drain. Discard the stems and thinly slice the caps. Combine with the other filling ingredients and set aside. Combine the sauce ingredients in a small bowl.

2. Cut the salmon in half to make 2 equal pieces, each about 3 inches wide. Split each piece horizontally almost all the way through, leaving one long edge attached; open it up like a book. Place half of the filling ingredients inside each piece of the salmon, then close like a book. Sprinkle the salmon with the salt, pepper and sesame oil.

3. Heat a wide frying pan over medium heat until hot. Add the cooking oil. Place the fish in the pan skin side up and cook for 2 minutes. Turn and cook 2 minutes on the other side. Add the sauce to the pan. Cover and simmer until the fish is opaque, 2 to 3 minutes.

4. With a slotted spatula, transfer the fish to a platter. Strain the sauce into a small pan and heat over medium-high heat. Add the cornstarch solution and cook, stirring, until the sauce boils and thickens. Pour the sauce over the fish and garnish with the lemon wedges. To serve, cut each portion of fish in half.

Grilled Mahi-Mahi with Fresh Papaya Salsa

Papaya Salsa

1 small papaya, peeled, seeded, and finely chopped

1 Asian pear, peeled, cored, and finely chopped

2 kiwifruit, peeled and finely chopped

¼ cup finely chopped red bell pepper

2 tablespoons chopped cilantro

1 tablespoon finely chopped red onion

1 teaspoon minced jalapeño or serrano chile

1 teaspoon minced ginger

2 tablespoons lime juice

2 tablespoons Chinese plum sauce

1 tablespoon soy sauce

❀

1½ to 2 pounds boned and skinned mahi-mahi, halibut, or other firm-fleshed fish, about 1 inch thick

1 tablespoon olive oil

Salt and pepper

Real freshness is what a true Chinese gourmand will demand when eating fish. The delicate flavor of fish grilled to perfection and a refreshing fruit salsa add up to a tantalizing winner. I use mahi-mahi, but you can use any fresh catch of the day. Let's go fishing!

Serves 4

1. Combine the salsa ingredients in a bowl; mix well. Cover and refrigerate until ready to serve.

2. Brush the fish on all sides with the oil, then sprinkle lightly with salt and pepper. Place the fish on an oiled grill 4 to 6 inches over a solid bed of hot glowing coals. Cook, turning once with a wide metal spatula, until the fish is opaque but still moist-looking in the thickest part, about 10 minutes. Transfer the fish to a warm platter. Serve the salsa on the side.

Steamed Snapper with Miso Sauce

4 green onions, cut in half
1 pound snapper or cod
    fillets, cut into 4 equal
    portions

Miso Sauce
⅓ cup rice vinegar
¼ cup mirin (Japanese sweet
    rice wine)
3 tablespoons white miso
1 tablespoon sugar
2 teaspoons grated ginger
1 teaspoon toasted sesame
    seeds
✿
½ pound broccoli florets,
    steamed or blanched

Fermented soybean products are widely used in Japanese and Chinese dishes as flavoring agents. Miso adds great taste and character to soups, salad dressings, and sauces for seafood. In fact, it goes well with any fish.

Serves 4

1. Place the green onion halves in a 9-inch heatproof glass pie pan. Place the fish over the green onions. Set the pan on a rack in a steamer, cover, and steam until the center of the fish is opaque, about 8 minutes.

2. While the fish is steaming, prepare the sauce: In a small pan, whisk together the rice vinegar, mirin, miso, sugar, ginger, and sesame seeds until smooth. Place over low heat and simmer for 2 minutes.

3. Pour the miso sauce onto a platter. Lift the fish from the pan with a slotted spatula and place it on top of the sauce; discard the green onions. Serve with steamed broccoli.

TIP: Laying the fish fillets on a bed of green onions allows the steam to circulate freely to cook the fish uniformly. Do the same with any whole fish.

 Japan is the disposable chopsticks capital of the world. More than half of all disposable chopsticks come from Japan—about 20 to 25 billion every year! If you laid them end to end, they'd stretch almost 2½ million miles!

Grilled Fish in a Banana Leaf

Marinade

2 tablespoons fish sauce
2 teaspoons lime juice
1 teaspoon cooking oil
2 tablespoons finely chopped
    shallots
1 tablespoon finely chopped
    cilantro
1 tablespoon minced garlic
1 teaspoon minced ginger
¼ teaspoon salt
Pinch of black pepper

❀

1 to 1½ pounds firm white
    fish fillets or steaks,
    about ¾ inch thick
1 banana leaf, thawed if
    frozen
6 fresh Thai basil or regular
    basil leaves, thinly sliced
Lime wedges

When I was growing up in China, we didn't have aluminum foil; we used lotus leaves and bamboo leaves to wrap and cook food. The people of India and Southeast Asia typically use banana leaves as wrappers for steamed and grilled foods. The leaves help retain the moisture in the food, while imparting a smoky taste and aroma — a heavenly marriage of flavors.

Serves 4

1. Combine the marinade ingredients in a medium bowl. Divide the fish into 4 portions, add to the marinade and stir to coat. Let stand for 15 minutes.

2. Cut the banana leaf into 4 pieces, each about 8 by 12 inches. Blanch in boiling water for 30 seconds or until soft; drain. Rinse with cold water and drain again.

3. Place the leaves, ribbed side up, on a clean work surface. Center a portion of fish on each leaf. Bring the 2 long sides of the leaf together and double fold to seal. Fasten the ends with wooden picks.

4. Place the packets on an oiled grill 4 to 6 inches over a solid bed of medium glowing coals. Grill until the fish is opaque, about 8 minutes on each side (carefully open a package to check doneness). If the leaf begins to burn, move it to a cooler spot on the grill.

5. Place the packets on a serving platter or individual dishes. Cut the packets open with scissors and scatter the basil over the fish. Serve the fish directly from the banana leaves, with lime wedges on the side.

TIP: Frozen banana leaves are available in many Asian stores. Simply cut off the length you want, wrap the unused portion in plastic, and return it to the freezer.

VARIATION: Place the fish packets in a single layer in a shallow baking pan and bake in a preheated 450°F oven for 10 minutes.

Seafood Shabu-Shabu

½ pound salmon fillet, skinned and thinly sliced
¼ pound medium raw shrimp, peeled and deveined
¼ pound bay scallops
8 ounces regular tofu, drained and cut into 1-inch squares
1 bunch spinach, leaves only
1 bunch watercress, heavy stems removed
6 green onions, cut diagonally into 1½-inch slices
2 ounces snow peas, ends and strings removed
1 can (8 ounces) bamboo shoots, thinly sliced
4 ounces enoki or other fresh mushrooms
8 ounces fresh udon noodles

Dipping Sauce
⅓ cup soy sauce
3 tablespoons lemon juice
2 tablespoons rice vinegar
1 tablespoon mirin (Japanese sweet rice wine)
1 teaspoon grated lemon peel

Soup Broth
4 cups *dashi* (Japanese bonito fish stock) or 1 package (0.35 ounce) *hondashi* plus 4 cups water
2 tablespoons sake
1 tablespoon sugar

To eat this Japanese specialty, the diners must become the cooks. As with fondue or a Mongolian firepot, each person picks out a bite of food with chopsticks (or a fondue fork), cooks it in the steaming broth, then dips it in the lemon-spiked sauce before eating. Plump noodles simmered in the enriched broth are a bonus at the end of this meal. Use the recipe just as a simple guideline; you can cook just about any seafood or vegetable in the broth as long as it is cut into small pieces. It is a leisurely meal for a sociable occasion or family gathering.

Serves 4

1. Arrange all the ingredients except the dipping sauce and soup broth attractively on a large platter, keeping each item separate. Cover and refrigerate until ready to cook. Combine the dipping sauce ingredients and pour into 4 small sauce bowls.

2. Bring the soup broth ingredients to a boil in a pan. At the table, pour the broth into a flameproof casserole set on a heating unit or into an electric wok or electric frying pan. Adjust the heat so the broth simmers gently. Place the platter of ingredients next to the cooking vessel and place a dipping sauce bowl next to each diner's plate. Starting with the seafood and vegetables, each diner cooks his or her choice of ingredients and seasons it with the dipping sauce.

3. When all the seafood and vegetables are cooked and served, add the noodles to the broth and cook until heated through. Ladle the noodles and broth into 4 soup bowls and serve.

TIP: *Dashi* is a distinctively flavored Japanese soup stock made of dried bonito (a small tuna) and seaweed. Available in powder *(dashi-no-moto),* liquid *(katsuo dashi),* and granular forms *(hon-dashi),* it comes in small packets or jars, and also in a tea bag form that dissolves quickly in warm water. If none is available, use chicken broth.

Seafood Bean Curd Rolls

Marinade

2 tablespoons dry white wine
1 tablespoon cornstarch
1 teaspoon minced ginger
¾ teaspoon salt
¼ teaspoon white pepper
1 whole egg or 2 egg whites,
    lightly beaten

❀

½ pound medium raw
    shrimp, peeled, split
    lengthwise, and deveined
½ pound firm white fish
    fillet such as sea bass or
    halibut, thinly sliced
    crosswise
1 large (24 inches in
    diameter) dried bean
    curd sheet, thawed if
    frozen
½ cup finely julienned
    bamboo shoots
1 small carrot, finely
    julienned
4 green onions, cut into 2-
    inch lengths and slivered
¼ cup cilantro leaves
2 sheets nori (Japanese
    roasted seaweed), cut
    into 2-inch-wide strips
2 tablespoons cooking oil
¼ cup chicken broth
Worcestershire sauce or bottled
    sweet and sour sauce

I don't know of many Chinese restaurants that don't have egg rolls or spring rolls on the menu. It seems to be everybody's favorite, but not mine. I love these stuffed bean curd rolls even more. Not only are they tasty, but they're not deep-fried. So I can eat as many as I like without having to worry about extra calories.

Serves 6

1. Combine the marinade ingredients in a medium bowl. Add the shrimp and fish and stir to coat. Let stand for 15 minutes.

2. Cut the bean curd sheet into 6 equal pie-shape pieces. To make each roll, dip a piece of the bean curd in cold water, drain, and place on a work surface with the point away from you. Place 1/6 of the shrimp, fish, bamboo shoots, carrot, green onions, and cilantro in a band across the near side, 1 inch in from the edge. Fold the bottom edge over the filling and fold in the sides. Moisten the edges of the bean curd with a dab of the marinade, then roll into a cylinder, pressing the edges to seal. Wrap a strip of the nori around the middle of the roll; overlap the ends, moisten with water, and press to seal.

3. Heat the cooking oil in a wide nonstick frying pan over medium-high heat until hot. Place the rolls in the pan and cook until golden brown, about 2 minutes on each side. Add the chicken broth, cover, and simmer for 3 minutes. Uncover and cook until the pan juices have almost evaporated. Turn the rolls and continue to cook for 1 minute. Cut the rolls in half diagonally and arrange on a serving platter. Serve with the Worcestershire sauce or sweet and sour sauce for dipping.

TIPS: If you want more texture and body add julienned celery to the filling.

    Bean curd sheet is a byproduct of tofu manufacture, the thin layer that forms on top of the soy milk as it cools.

It is sold either dried or in soft form. The dried form will keep for several months in a cool, dry place and needs to be soaked in water until pliable. The soft variety will keep in the freezer for months, and just needs to be moistened before rolling.

Thai Shrimp with Red Curry Paste

2 tablespoons cooking oil
2 tablespoons minced garlic
1 jalapeño or serrano chile, thinly sliced
1 small onion, cut into 1-inch squares
1 green bell pepper, seeded and cut into 1-inch squares
⅓ cup chicken broth
2 tablespoons Red Curry Paste (see below)
¾ pound raw medium shrimp, peeled and deveined

Curry pastes of various colors and flavors are essential in many Thai dishes. This one uses a basic red curry paste, made with dried red chiles and other ingredients found in well-stocked Asian markets. The curry paste recipe here makes enough for several dishes and will keep in the refrigerator for several weeks if stored in an airtight jar. Once you have the curry paste made, you can make a fragrant, flavorful curry of shrimp or other seafood or meats in a few minutes.

Serves 4

1. Heat a wok over high heat until hot. Add the cooking oil, garlic, and chile and stir-fry for 30 seconds. Add the onion, bell pepper, chicken broth, and curry paste; cook, stirring, for 3 minutes.

2. Add the shrimp to the wok and stir-fry for 2 to 3 minutes, or until the shrimp turn pink. Serve with cooked rice.

Red Curry Paste

16 whole dried chile peppers
4 quarter-size slices dried galangal
4 strips dried kaffir lime rind
3 stalks lemongrass

1. Cut off the stem ends of the chiles and shake out the seeds. Soak the chiles, galangal, and lime rind in separate bowls of warm water for 30 minutes, or until soft and pliable; drain.

2. Remove the loose outer leaves of the lemongrass until you reach the tighter ones inside; cut off the bottom. Slice the bottom 6 inches of the stalk crosswise into

1 teaspoon whole coriander
   seeds (or ½ teaspoon
   ground)
1 teaspoon whole black
   peppercorns
½ teaspoon whole cumin
   seeds
5 cloves garlic, chopped
3 small shallots
2 cilantro roots, chopped
2 teaspoons shrimp paste
Salt to taste
2 tablespoons water

very thin slices, then chop. Discard the top.

3. Toast the coriander seeds, peppercorns, and cumin seeds in a small ungreased skillet over medium heat until fragrant, about 2 or 3 minutes.

4. In a mini-food processor or spice grinder, chop the lemongrass as fine as possible. Add the toasted spices and process until fine. Add the chiles, galangal, and lime rind and process as fine as possible. Add the garlic, shallots, cilantro roots, shrimp paste, and salt. Process to a fine paste, adding enough water to facilitate the processing. (This may have to be done in several batches.) Remove to a small bowl; mix well. Store in a clean airtight jar in the refrigerator.

TIP: Traditionally curry pastes are pounded together in a heavy stone mortar with a pestle until all the ingredients become a very fine paste. This is undoubtedly the best tool for extracting the oils, juices, and flavors of the galangal, kaffir lime rind, shallots, and other fresh herbs and spices, but it takes a lot of time and energy. It's much easier and more convenient to use a mini-processor or spice grinder. The sharpness of the blade and the power of the processor will determine the smoothness of the paste, so make sure your blades are sharp. You might have greater success if you process each ingredient separately instead of crowding the ingredients into the machine all at once. After processing individually, combine all the ingredients to form a homogeneous paste. This method will take a little more time, but you will be rewarded with a better textured and flavored paste in the end.

Vietnamese Bouillabaisse

Stock

2 tablespoons olive oil
1 medium onion, chopped
3 tablespoons minced shallots
1 tablespoon minced garlic
1 jalapeño or serrano chile,
    thinly sliced
2 cups chicken broth
1 cup water
1 bottle (8 ounces) clam juice
1 cup dry white wine
3 tablespoons fish sauce
1 stalk lemongrass, bottom 6
    inches, lightly crushed

❀

18 small hard-shell clams,
    well scrubbed
½ pound medium raw
    shrimp, deveined but not
    peeled
½ pound firm white fish,
    skinned, boned, and cut
    into bite-size pieces
1 cup chopped peeled
    tomatoes
2 green onions, thinly sliced
2 tablespoons shredded fresh
    basil leaves
2 tablespoons shredded fresh
    mint leaves
1 teaspoon sesame oil

When the French settled in Vietnam, they brought with them bouillabaisse, the famous fish stew from Marseilles. The Vietnamese quickly made it their own by adding their favorite local ingredients such as shallots, chiles, lemongrass, basil, and mint. What a tasty blend of international cuisines! Serve this with crusty French bread to dunk in the fragrant broth.

Serves 4

1. Prepare the stock: Heat the olive oil in a 5-quart pan over medium-high heat until hot. Add the onion, shallots, garlic, and chile and cook for 2 minutes. Add the chicken broth, water, clam juice, wine, fish sauce, and lemongrass. Bring to a boil, reduce the heat, cover, and simmer for 30 minutes. Remove the lemongrass.

2. Add the clams, shrimp, and fish. Cover and simmer until the clams open and the shrimp turn pink, about 10 minutes. Add the tomatoes, green onions, basil, and mint and cook for 1 minute. Stir in the sesame oil. As you serve the soup, discard any unopened clams.

TIP: Soaking the clams in water for 2 hours then scrubbing them with a stiff-bristled brush will get rid of most of the sand that is trapped on the shells. To eliminate all traces of sand, I like to blanch the raw clams in a pot of hot water for 30 seconds before adding them to the soup.

Singapore Chili Crab

1 live Dungeness crab (1¾ to 2 pounds)

Sauce
⅓ cup tomato sauce
2 teaspoons Chinese chili sauce
2 teaspoons soy sauce
2 teaspoons sugar

❀

3 tablespoons cooking oil
8 to 10 whole dried chile peppers
1 jalapeño or serrano chile, thinly sliced
1 tablespoon minced garlic
1 tablespoon minced ginger
⅔ cup chicken broth
2 green onions, cut in half diagonally

If you ever visit Singapore, the cleanest and most orderly city in the world, you are sure to be introduced to their national dish, chili crab. You can walk into any specialty seafood restaurant, and this will be the first dish your host will serve. Make this fiery specialty at home with any hard-shell crab—Dungeness, blue, even snow crab legs or stone crab claws. Cooked in the shell, it's a bit messy to eat, but worth every succulent bite. Don't forget to savor the tasty sauce on the shell before you dig into the meat.

Serves 4

1. Bring a large pot of water to a boil. Immerse the live crab and cook for 2 to 3 minutes. Drain and cool quickly with cold running water. Pull off the top shell in one piece and reserve. Remove and discard the gills and spongy parts under the shell. Twist off the claws and legs. With a cleaver, cut the body into six parts.

2. Combine the sauce ingredients in a small bowl.

3. Heat a wok over high heat until hot. Add the oil and dried and fresh chiles and stir-fry for 30 seconds. Add the crab pieces and stir-fry for 1 minute. Add the garlic and ginger and stir-fry for 1 minute. Add the chicken broth and cover with the top shell. Cover and cook until the crab is cooked through and the top shell is bright red, about 3 minutes. Remove and reserve the top shell. Add the sauce and cook until the crab is nicely glazed, about 1 minute.

4. Arrange the crab legs and body pieces on a platter. Set the top shell and green onions on top as a garnish.

TIP: If you are shopping within an hour or two of cooking time, you might ask the fishmonger to kill and clean the crab for you and skip the boiling part of step 1. Don't forget to save the whole top shell for the best presentation.

100

Jumbo Shrimp with Cantaloupe

Marinade

½ teaspoon salt
¼ teaspoon white pepper
2 teaspoons cornstarch

✿

¾ pound jumbo raw shrimp, peeled, deveined, and cut in half lengthwise

Sauce

3 tablespoons lemon juice
2 tablespoons chicken broth
2 tablespoons plum wine
2 teaspoons sugar
Salt to taste

✿

1 tablespoon cooking oil
2 cups ¾-inch cantaloupe balls
2 teaspoons cornstarch dissolved in 4 teaspoons water
Grated lemon peel
Mint leaves

Fresh seasonal fruits are a perfect compliment to meat and seafoods and they are being incorporated into stir-fried dishes by many Chinese chefs. I use juicy California Westside cantaloupe to add texture, fragrance, and a delicately sweet touch to tender stir-fried shrimp.

Serves 4

1. Combine the marinade ingredients in a medium bowl. Add the shrimp and stir to coat. Let stand for 30 minutes. Combine the sauce ingredients in a small bowl.

2. Heat a wok over medium-high heat until hot. Add the oil and shrimp and stir-fry for 1 minute or until the shrimp turn pink. Add the cantaloupe and sauce and cook for 2 minutes. Add the cornstarch solution and cook, stirring, until the sauce boils and thickens. Garnish with the lemon peel and mint leaves.

TIP: Cantaloupe grown on the west side of the San Joaquin Valley of California is at its best from July to September. It is easy to select a good ripe melon—just follow your nose to one with a sweet, fragrant, and musky smell. It should be without dents and bruises. If it rattles (from the seeds sloshing inside) when shaken, it may be overripe.

In Japan, chopsticks are so important that a special holiday is set aside to honor them. Every year, on August 4th, people come from all over the country to attend a ceremony in which chopsticks are burned as a sign of gratitude for their use.

Sauteed Shrimp in Chili-Tomato Sauce

¼ teaspoon salt
1 tablespoon dry sherry
1 tablespoon cornstarch
1 pound raw jumbo shrimp, peeled, deveined, and butterflied

Sauce

¼ cup catsup
2 tablespoons hoisin sauce
1 teaspoon Worcestershire sauce
1 teaspoon sesame oil
1 tablespoon shredded fresh basil leaves

✿

2 tablespoons cooking oil
2 tablespoons chopped onion
2 teaspoons minced garlic
2 teaspoons minced ginger
½ teaspoon crushed red pepper

If you've ever eaten in Hong Kong, the "fragrant harbor" of Asia, or in any Hong Kong-style seafood restaurant in this country, you probably saw this on the menu. It is one of the most popular dishes among the Chinese and is amazingly easy to prepare in your own kitchen.

Serves 4

1. Combine the salt, sherry, and cornstarch in a medium bowl. Add the shrimp, stir to coat, and let stand for 30 minutes. Combine the sauce ingredients in a small bowl.

2. Heat a wok over high heat until hot. Add the oil, onion, garlic, ginger and red pepper; cook for 30 seconds. Add the shrimp and stir-fry until pink, 2 to 3 minutes. Add the sauce and cook for 1 minute or until the shrimp are nicely glazed.

TIP: Traditionally, restaurants cook and serve these shrimp with the shells left on. In this recipe, I've made it easy for you, but try preparing the dish with the shells left on at least once. You'll find the flavor is even more intense and juicy with the added crunchy texture of the shells.

In Chinese folklore, if you hold your chopsticks near the tip, it means you will marry close to home. If held high, you will marry far from home.

Shrimp and Egg Scramble

1 teaspoon cornstarch
½ teaspoon salt
⅛ teaspoon white pepper
½ pound raw medium
    shrimp, peeled, split
    lengthwise, and deveined
2 tablespoons cooking oil
1 teaspoon finely minced
    ginger
2 tablespoons chopped onion
¼ cup frozen green peas,
    thawed
1 teaspoon sesame oil
3 eggs, lightly beaten
Pinch of salt
¼ teaspoon toasted black
    sesame seeds

You will find this kind of scrambled egg dish not only in most Chinese households but also in many Chinese restaurants. From cooktop to table, all it takes is 5 minutes to prepare.

Serves 4

1. Combine the cornstarch, salt, and pepper in a medium bowl. Add the shrimp and stir to coat. Let stand for 30 minutes.

2. Heat a wok or nonstick frying pan over high heat. Add 1 tablespoon of the cooking oil and the ginger and onion and cook for 1 minute. Add the shrimp and cook for 2 minutes or until pink. Add the peas and sesame oil and cook for 30 seconds. Remove the shrimp mixture from the pan.

3. Add the remaining tablespoon of oil to the pan. Add the eggs and lightly scramble for 30 seconds. Return the shrimp mixture and add the salt; gently toss for 30 seconds. Sprinkle with sesame seeds and serve.

TIP: The eggs should not be over-stirred like American scrambled eggs often are. Allow a cooked layer to form around the edges before stirring gently toward the center to form large, soft, moist curds.

Shrimp Curry Cooked in a Coconut

¼ cup coconut milk
1 tablespoon fish sauce
2 tablespoons minced shallots
1 small jalapeño or serrano chile, minced
2 teaspoons curry powder
½ teaspoon sugar
¼ teaspoon turmeric
½ pound medium raw shrimp, peeled and deveined
1 large coconut
2 fresh Thai basil or regular basil leaves, julienned

This is a simple and impressive dish you can prepare for special occasions or just for an everyday meal. When I have guests, I serve the shrimp as an appetizer in a stunning coconut shell. When I prepare it for my family, I enjoy it as an entree served over steamed rice. It's always delicious, no matter your choice of company.

Serves 2

1. Combine the coconut milk, fish sauce, shallots, chile, curry powder, sugar, and turmeric in a bowl. Add the shrimp, stir to coat, and let stand for 15 minutes.

2. Preheat the oven to 350°F. Punch holes in the eyes of the coconut with an icepick or other clean tool. Drain off and discard the water inside. Remove about the top third of the coconut with a saw or a strong serrated knife. Spoon the uncooked shrimp mixture into the coconut and cover tightly with foil. Stand the coconut in a small pie pan and bake until the shrimp turn completely pink, 1¼ to 1½ hours. Uncover and stir several times during cooking. Serve from the shell, garnished with basil.

TIP: Baking the curry in the coconut takes a lot of patience, because the heat takes a long time to penetrate the thick coconut shell and meat. But the result is a tender, succulent dish with a delicate coconut flavor. If you don't have the time, you can bake the curry in a small covered casserole in 25 to 30 minutes; it will still be delicious.

Sauteed Shrimp with Glazed Walnuts

¾ pound medium raw
  shrimp

Marinade

1 tablespoon Chinese rice
  wine or dry sherry
2 teaspoons cornstarch
½ teaspoon salt
⅛ teaspoon white pepper

Sauce

⅓ cup mayonnaise
1 teaspoon sugar
2 teaspoons grated lemon
  peel
1 teaspoon sesame oil
½ teaspoon salt

✿

2 tablespoons cooking oil
2 tablespoons chicken broth
1½ cups Candied Walnuts
  (see page 179)

Those who have visited Hong Kong in recent years will have seen this dish on many Chinese restaurant menus. It is a dish created by the new generation of Chinese chefs who are practitioners of fusion cuisine. The sauce gets its unique flavor and a velvety smooth consistency from a very un-Chinese ingredient—mayonnaise.

Serves 4

1. Peel the shrimp. Split each shrimp along the back, cutting almost through to make the shrimp lie flat; devein the shrimp. Rinse and dry with paper towels.

2. Combine the marinade ingredients in a medium bowl. Add the shrimp, stir to coat, and let stand for 30 minutes. Combine the sauce ingredients in a small bowl.

3. Heat a wok over high heat until hot. Add the cooking oil and shrimp and stir-fry until the shrimp turn pink, about 1½ minutes. Add the chicken broth and cook for 30 seconds. Add the sauce and cook for 30 seconds or until the sauce is heated through. Sprinkle with the walnuts and serve.

106

Poultry
and
Meats

Three-Cup Drumsticks

2 tablespoons cooking oil
8 chicken drumsticks
4 cloves garlic, lightly crushed
8 thin slices ginger, lightly crushed
5 whole dried chile peppers
1 cup water
1 cup Shao Hsing wine or dry sherry
½ cup dark soy sauce
½ cup regular soy sauce
4 ounces rock sugar or ⅓ cup granulated sugar
2 tablespoons sesame oil
2 green onions, cut in half

This is a classic "red-cooked" dish commonly found in northern China. Traditionally, one cup each of soy sauce, sesame oil, and Shao Hsing wine is used in this recipe. I prefer to use a little sesame oil just for flavor and water instead of wine for a lighter taste. A blend of soy sauces makes for a smoother, richer flavor. Save the cooking liquid as a "master sauce" for future stewing and braising.

Serves 4

1. Heat a wok over medium-high heat until hot. Add the cooking oil and brown the chicken on all sides. Remove the chicken from the wok. Discard all but 1 tablespoon of the oil.

2. Increase the heat to high. Add the garlic, ginger, and chiles and stir-fry for 1 minute. Add the water, wine, soy sauces, sugar, sesame oil, and green onions. Return the chicken to the wok and bring to a boil. Stir to coat the chicken. Reduce the heat to low, cover, and simmer until the meat is no longer pink, about 20 minutes.

3. Lift out the chicken with a slotted spoon, drain briefly, and place on a serving platter. Serve with some of the sauce. Reserve the remaining sauce as a master sauce. Serve hot or cold.

TIP: Other parts of the chicken, such as the thighs or wings, may be substituted for the drumsticks. You can also skin the chicken before browning.

General Tso's Chicken

Marinade
2 tablespoons Shao Hsing
    wine
1 tablespoon dark soy sauce
2 teaspoons cornstarch
❀
1 pound boneless, skinless
    chicken, cut into 1-inch
    pieces

Sauce
2 tablespoons chicken broth
1 tablespoon rice vinegar
1 tablespoon regular soy
    sauce
2 teaspoons dark soy sauce
1 teaspoon sesame oil
2 teaspoons sugar
❀
2 tablespoons peanut oil
8 whole dried chile peppers
2 teaspoons minced garlic
1 teaspoon minced ginger
1 green onion, cut into 1-
    inch pieces
¼ teaspoon crushed red
    pepper
¾ cup roasted unsalted
    peanuts
1 teaspoon cornstarch
    dissolved in 2 teaspoons
    water

There are as many versions of General Tso's Chicken (named after a famous general from Hunan province hundreds of years ago) as there are Chinese chefs. Most restaurants deep-fry boneless pieces of chicken. My stir-fried version is simpler, quicker, healthier, and just as delicious. For additional flavor, texture, and protein, I've added roasted unsalted peanuts.

Serves 4

1. Combine the marinade ingredients in a medium bowl. Add the chicken and stir to coat. Let stand for 30 minutes. Combine the sauce ingredients in a small bowl.

2. Heat a wok over high heat until hot. Add the oil and chiles and stir-fry until the chiles darken to a deep red, about 10 seconds. Add the chicken and stir-fry for 2 minutes. Add the garlic, ginger, green onion, and crushed red pepper; stir-fry for 1 minute. Add the sauce and peanuts and cook, stirring, for 1 minute. Add the cornstarch solution and cook, stirring, until the sauce thickens and the chicken is nicely glazed.

TIPS: Although it seems that using 8 whole chile peppers in this dish is excessive, this amount of chile will produce only a medium-hot dish. The reason you can use so many whole chile peppers compared to crushed red peppers is because the seeds and inside ribs of the chiles, which have all the heat and fire, are not exposed to the oil or liquid in the dish. The whole chiles are included just for their flavor and color; they are not intended to be eaten, unless you really enjoy a hot burning mouth!

Peanut oil is preferred by many Chinese chefs for its high smoking point and unique flavor-sealing qualities. Even if you usually use another oil for stir-frying, in this dish you might want to try using peanut oil; its higher cooking temperature will help seal in the chicken juices and will also give the chicken a nice golden color.

Roast Chicken with Black Rice Stuffing

½ cup dried chestnuts
6 dried black mushrooms
2 cups uncooked black glutinous rice
2 tablespoons cooking oil
4 shallots, thinly sliced
1 Chinese sausage (about 2 ounces), thinly sliced diagonally
2 green onions, thinly sliced
3 tablespoons oyster sauce
1 teaspoon sesame oil
½ cup chopped pitted dates
6 hard-boiled quail eggs
½ teaspoon salt
½ teaspoon Chinese five-spice
2 tablespoons soy sauce
½ teaspoon white pepper
1 roasting chicken, 4 to 5 pounds, giblets removed

Try this in place of your traditional Thanksgiving turkey feast. Your guests will be in awe over the color contrast of the black rice stuffing, which flows out of a tender, juicy, golden brown roast chicken. A striking purplish color when cooked, black rice has a flavor that closely resembles that of wild rice.

Serves 6

1. Soak the dried chestnuts overnight in water to cover; drain. Place them in a pan and cover with fresh water. Simmer, covered, until soft, about 30 minutes; drain. Soak the mushrooms in warm water for 30 minutes; drain. Discard the stems and thinly slice the caps.

2. Rinse and drain the rice; place it in a 2-quart pan with 2¼ cups of water. Bring to a boil, uncovered, and boil until the water is reduced to the level of the rice. Reduce the heat, cover, and simmer until the rice is tender, 15 to 20 minutes. Uncover, drain, and cool briefly.

3. Heat a wok over medium-high heat until hot. Add the cooking oil, shallots, sausage, and dried mushrooms and stir-fry for 1 minute. Reduce the heat to medium. Add the chestnuts and rice and cook, stirring, for 1 minute. Add the green onions and oyster sauce and cook for 1 minute. Stir in ½ teaspoon of the sesame oil. Remove the wok from the heat; add the dates and quail eggs and toss lightly to mix. Let cool.

4. Preheat the oven to 400°F. Rub the salt and five-spice all over the inside and outside of the chicken. Rub the soy sauce and pepper over the skin. Spoon the stuffing into the chicken. Skewer the opening closed. Place the chicken, breast side up, on a rack in a shallow roasting pan. Bake, uncovered, for 20 minutes. Reduce the heat to 350°F. Continue to cook until the meat near the thigh bone is no longer pink when pierced, 1¼ to 1½ hours. Remove from the oven and brush it with the remaining sesame oil. Let stand 10 minutes before carving.

TIP: Any leftover stuffing can be baked in an oiled, covered baking dish during the last 30 minutes of roasting time.

When a good ingredient is available, use it. One great ingredient is the California Medjool date. It's available all year round and packed with vitamins and minerals. Choose glossy, plump dates when buying.

Roast Duck with Papaya-Ginger Glaze

1 duckling, 4 to 5 pounds, cleaned

Marinade
2 tablespoons soy sauce
1 tablespoon dry sherry
2 teaspoons minced ginger
½ teaspoon sesame oil
¼ teaspoon Chinese five-spice
Pinch of white pepper

Glaze
½ medium papaya, peeled and seeded
¼ cup chicken broth
2 tablespoons honey
1 tablespoon candied ginger

I can't imagine a more delicious way to serve roast duckling than with this savory-sweet glaze. The thick and creamy pulp from the papaya blends together with honey and caramelizes when baked, resulting in a golden brown crackling skin and incredibly tender, juicy meat. This is one of my favorite recipes when I entertain friends.

Serves 4 to 6

1. *One day ahead,* cut off and discard the excess neck skin and tail from the duck. Remove all loose fat and prick the skin around the legs and breast with a small sharp knife. Be careful not to pierce the meat underneath. Combine the marinade ingredients in a large bowl. Add the duck and rub it inside and out with the marinade. Cover and refrigerate overnight.

2. Place a steaming rack in a wok. Pour in water to just below the level of the rack and bring to a boil. Place the duck on the rack, cover, and steam for 30 minutes to remove the excess fat. Cool slightly. While the duck cools, preheat the oven to 375°F.

3. Place the duck, breast side down, on a rack in a foil-lined baking pan. Bake, uncovered, for 1 hour. Meanwhile, process the glaze ingredients in a food processor until smooth. Brush the duck with the glaze and bake until the glaze caramelizes, about 12 minutes.

Poached Whole Cantonese Chicken

3 tablespoons dry sherry
2 teaspoons salt
1 teaspoon minced ginger
1 teaspoon minced garlic
1 frying chicken (about 3 to 4 pounds), giblets removed

Poaching liquid
3 quarts water
6 thin slices ginger, lightly crushed
2 green onions

Dipping Sauce
¼ cup cooking oil
1 teaspoon minced garlic
1 teaspoon minced jalapeño or serrano chile
2 green onions, thinly sliced
2 tablespoons minced ginger
1 teaspoon salt
¼ teaspoon crushed red pepper
Pinch of Chinese five-spice
✿
1 teaspoon sesame oil

In this book and in the current Yan Can Cook show, I like to introduce favorite family dishes served in homes and at restaurants. This is one that many of my Chinese friends order when they go out to eat. It is an amazingly simple dish to prepare. Serve the chicken hot or chilled with the delectable dipping sauce.

Serves 4 to 6

1. Combine the sherry, salt, ginger, and garlic in a deep bowl. Add the chicken and rub the sherry mixture on all sides. Cover and refrigerate for 2 hours.

2. Bring the poaching liquid ingredients to a boil in a 5-quart pot and boil for 5 minutes. Add the chicken and cover the pot. When the liquid returns to a boil, reduce the heat and simmer for 30 minutes. Turn off the heat and let the chicken stand in the poaching liquid, covered, for 15 minutes.

3. Meanwhile, prepare the dipping sauce: Heat the oil in a small pan until hot. Add the garlic and chile and stir-fry for 30 seconds. Remove the pan from the heat, add the remaining sauce ingredients, and mix well.

4. Lift out the chicken, drain briefly, and place on a plate. Let stand for 10 minutes, then brush with the sesame oil.

5. To serve, cut the chicken through the bone with a heavy cleaver into 1- by 2-inch pieces. Arrange the chicken on a serving plate. Or, if you wish, bone the chicken and cut the meat into bite-size pieces. Place the chicken in a deep bowl and press down to make a compact layer. Cover the bowl with a plate and invert so the chicken forms a mound. Serve the dipping sauce in a separate bowl or spoon the sauce over the chicken.

Beggar's Cornish Game Hen

Marinade

2 tablespoons soy sauce
2 tablespoons dry sherry or
    Chinese rice wine
1 tablespoon dark soy sauce
2 teaspoons minced ginger
1 teaspoon sesame oil

✿

2 Cornish game hens (about
    1½ pounds each), giblets
    removed
4 lotus leaves or 2 18-inch
    squares heavy duty foil

Stuffing

2 tablespoons preserved
    turnip leaves (dong choy)
2 green onions, thinly sliced
1 rib celery, finely chopped
¼ cup roasted unsalted
    peanuts

Baker's Clay

8 cups all-purpose flour
8 cups salt
4 cups water

One of the most widely told folk tales in China tells of a beggar who stole a chicken from a farmer, then fled to the riverbank to escape capture. Like most folk tales, it has many different versions. One says he buried his chicken in the mud, where it baked in the sun as he hid out from his pursuers. Another says he encased the chicken in mud and stashed it in his fire. Other versions offer other variations, but they all agree on one thing: when it was safe to return, he found the chicken cooked to perfection inside its clay shell.

Whichever version you have heard, Beggar's Chicken is a Chinese classic. Cooking the chicken (or in this case, two Cornish hens) in a shell of lotus leaves and pastry produces a tender juicy reward—and will have your family and guests begging for more.

Serves 2 to 4

1. Combine the marinade ingredients in a large bowl. Rub the hens inside and out with marinade. Pour the excess marinade into the cavities. Cover and refrigerate for 2 hours.

2. If using lotus leaves, place them in a large 2- to 3-inch-deep roasting pan. Pour boiling water over the leaves to cover. Weigh down the leaves with a heatproof plate; keep the leaves submerged for 30 minutes. Place the pan over medium-low heat and simmer for 10 minutes; drain.

3. Combine the stuffing ingredients in a small bowl and stuff each hen with half of the stuffing.

4. Place 2 lotus leaves, rib side up, on a work surface, overlapping the leaves as necessary to cover any holes. Center one hen on the leaves. Fold one side over the hen, then fold in the two adjacent sides. Fold over the fourth side and tuck in as if tucking in the flap of an envelope. If using foil, wrap each hen in foil so it is completely enclosed.

5. Prepare the baker's clay: Combine the flour and salt in a large bowl. Add the water to make a firm dough. Roll half of the dough out onto lightly floured parchment paper to ½ inch thick. Place a wrapped chicken in the center, and using the parchment paper to help you lift, bring the dough up and around the hen. Pinch the edges to seal.

6. Preheat the oven to 400°F. Place a rack large enough to hold both hens in a large roasting pan. Cover the rack with foil (this prevents the dough from sagging on the rack) and punch a few holes in the foil to allow the air to circulate under the rack. Place the hens on the rack and bake for 2 hours.

7. Remove the hens from the oven and transfer them to a cutting board. Break open the clay shell with a heavy cleaver or chef's knife; discard the shell. Transfer the hens to a platter and fold back the lotus leaves or foil. The meat should be very tender, almost falling off the bones.

TIP: Preserved turnip leaves (*dong choy*) are traditional in this dish. They are sold in some Asian markets in small earthenware pickling crocks, and should be rinsed in water and patted dry before using. Other Chinese preserved vegetables, though not exactly the same in flavor, can be used instead.

Chicken and Mushroom Purses

Marinade
1 tablespoon dry sherry or Chinese rice wine
2 teaspoons soy sauce
1 teaspoon cornstarch

❀

½ pound boneless, skinless chicken, coarsely chopped
4 dried black mushrooms

Sauce
3 tablespoons chicken broth
1 tablespoon hoisin sauce
1 tablespoon oyster sauce

❀

6 mu shu wrappers (available in Chinese markets)
2 tablespoons cooking oil
⅓ cup finely diced carrot
¼ cup finely diced water chestnuts
¼ cup thinly sliced Chinese chives or green onions
6 Chinese chives or green onion tops, blanched for 10 seconds

This versatile savory stuffing can go in all sorts of wrappers. For a handsome party presentation, wrap it in a steaming, moist mu shu wrapper or crepe and tie the purse with a chive.

Serves 6

1. Combine the marinade ingredients in a medium bowl. Add the chicken and stir to coat. Let stand for 30 minutes. Soak the mushrooms in warm water for 30 minutes; drain. Discard the stems and finely chop the caps. Combine the sauce ingredients in a small bowl.

2. Place the mu shu wrappers on a heatproof dish. Set the dish on a rack over boiling water in a wok. Cover and steam until hot, 4 to 5 minutes. Keep warm.

3. Heat a wok over high heat until hot. Add the oil and chicken and stir-fry for 1 minute. Add the carrot, water chestnuts, mushrooms, and chives and stir-fry for 1 minute. Add the sauce and cook for 30 seconds.

4. For each serving, place about 3 tablespoons of the chicken mixture in the center of a wrapper and gather it into a purse shape. Tie a chive or green onion top around each packet.

VARIATION: For a more casual approach, fold the wrappers burrito style, or for the kids, spoon the filling into pocket bread halves or sesame seed buns.

Curried Coconut Chicken

Sauce
1 cup coconut milk
⅓ cup chicken broth
¼ cup plum sauce
2 tablespoons fish sauce
2½ tablespoons curry
    powder
2 jalapeño or serrano chiles,
    minced

✿

1 tablespoon cooking oil
2½ pounds boneless chicken
    thighs, cut in half
1 medium onion, cut into 1-
    inch squares
1 tablespoon minced garlic
3 medium thin-skinned
    potatoes, cut into 1-inch
    chunks
¾ pound whole peeled baby
    carrots
2 pieces dried tangerine peel
    or 2 teaspoons grated
    orange peel
Salt to taste
3 tablespoons chopped fresh
    Thai or regular basil

Many Indian and Southeast Asian curries are served with sambals and chutneys as accompaniments on the side. My curry incorporates Chinese plum sauce, which adds its own fruity taste to the spicy blend. Please experiment with other fruits, nuts, and vegetables; let your imagination run wild and your taste buds indulge in the refreshing spicy, sweet flavors. Serve with steamed rice or a pilaf.

Serves 6

1. Combine the sauce ingredients in a medium bowl and whisk until evenly blended.

2. Heat the oil in a 5-quart pan over medium-high heat. Add the chicken and cook, turning once, until lightly browned on each side, about 5 minutes total. Remove the chicken from the pan. Discard all but 1 tablespoon of the pan drippings. Add the onion and cook for 1½ minutes. Add the garlic and cook for 10 seconds. Return the chicken to the pan; add the potatoes, carrots, tangerine peel, and sauce. Bring to a boil; reduce the heat, cover, and simmer until the chicken is no longer pink when cut in the thickest part, about 45 minutes. Add salt to taste. Stir in the basil just before serving.

TIP: Curries are delicious with chutneys of any kind. The Major Grey's type based on mangoes and raisins is only one of many types of chutneys found in India. Another popular accompaniment to curries is *raita,* a refreshing mixture of plain yogurt mixed with cucumber and tomato. It is used to cool the palate after eating savory curries. Curries may also be served with *naan,* a flat bread flavored with onions or sometimes raisins. These breads are commonly served in Indian restaurants.

Sizzling Chicken Fajitas

Marinade

2-inch piece dried tangerine
    peel *or* 2 teaspoons
    grated orange peel
¼ cup orange juice
3 tablespoons lime juice
3 tablespoons soy sauce
2 tablespoons dry sherry
2 tablespoons cooking oil
1 tablespoon minced jalapeño
    or serrano chile
2 teaspoons minced garlic
2 teaspoons grated ginger
1 teaspoon sugar
½ teaspoon ground cumin

❀

4 boneless, skinless chicken
    breast halves
8 to 12 small flour tortillas
2 tablespoons cooking oil
1 small jalapeño or serrano
    chile, minced
1 *each* red and yellow bell
    pepper, seeded and
    julienned
1 large carrot, julienned
1 small red onion, thinly
    sliced
1 or 2 avocados, peeled,
    pitted, and sliced
Roasted Sweet Pepper Salsa
    (see page 43)
Cilantro sprigs

How about a chicken fajita? Serve this sizzling hot at the table or simply layer the goodies in a tortilla and roll it up for everybody to enjoy. Either way, your guests will be singing praises for your creation. The fragrant citrus marinade leaves the chicken loaded with flavor.

Serves 4 to 6

1. Soak the tangerine peel in warm water for 30 minutes; drain and finely chop the peel. Place the peel in a bowl with the remaining marinade ingredients.

2. Place the breast halves between 2 sheets of plastic wrap and pound with a flat-surfaced mallet until about ¼ inch thick. Place the breasts in a sealable plastic bag, pour in the marinade, and seal the bag. Refrigerate for 2 or 4 hours; turn the bag occasionally to distribute marinade.

3. Lift the chicken from the marinade and drain briefly; reserve the marinade. Place the chicken on an oiled grill 4 to 6 inches above a solid bed of medium-glowing coals. Cook until the chicken is no longer pink when cut, about 3 minutes on each side. Meanwhile, stack and wrap the tortillas in foil and place on one side of the grill to heat.

4. While the chicken is grilling, heat a wok over high heat until hot. Add the oil, chile, bell peppers, carrot, and onion and stir-fry for 1 minute. Add ¼ cup of the reserved chicken marinade and stir-fry for 1 minute.

5. To serve, cut the chicken across the grain into slanting slices. Place the chicken, vegetables, and tortillas on a platter. Place the avocado, salsa, and cilantro sprigs in separate serving dishes. Wrap the chicken and your choice of condiments in a tortilla and eat out of hand.

Chicken and Asparagus with Black Bean Sauce

Along with ginger, soy sauce, and sesame oil, aromatic and pungent salted black beans are one of the most widely used ingredients in traditional Chinese dishes. Chicken with black bean sauce is one of the most popular dishes on the Chinese menu. I've added fresh California asparagus for its wonderful texture and delicate sweetness, which harmonize well with the salted black beans.

Serves 4

Marinade

1 tablespoon dry sherry
1 tablespoon soy sauce
2 teaspoons cornstarch

❀

¾ pound boneless, skinless chicken, thinly sliced
2 tablespoons cooking oil
1 tablespoon minced garlic
3 tablespoons salted black beans, rinsed, drained, and coarsely chopped
¾ pound asparagus, tough ends removed, thinly sliced diagonally
1 small onion, thinly sliced
½ cup chicken broth
1 medium red bell pepper, seeded and thinly sliced
1 teaspoon sugar
1 teaspoon cornstarch dissolved in 2 teaspoons water

1. Combine the marinade ingredients in a medium bowl. Add the chicken and stir to coat. Let stand for 30 minutes.

2. Heat a wok over high heat until hot. Add 1 tablespoon of the cooking oil and the chicken and stir-fry for 2 minutes. Remove the chicken from the wok. Add the remaining 1 tablespoon oil and the garlic and black beans and cook for 10 seconds. Add the asparagus, onion, and broth. Cover and cook for 2 minutes. Return the chicken to the wok. Add the bell pepper and sugar and stir-fry for 1 minute. Add the cornstarch solution and cook, stirring, until the sauce boils and thickens.

TIPS: Crushing black beans gives a stronger taste; leaving them whole will yield a milder flavor.

To prepare fresh asparagus, bend the stalks until they snap in two; discard the bases. Slicing asparagus at an angle decreases the length of the fibers and exposes more surface area, reducing the cooking time needed.

California asparagus is available from February to June, with peak supplies from March to May. It is low in calories and a great source of vitamins C and B6, potassium, and thiamin. When choosing asparagus, pick bright green spears with closed, compact, firm tips. Slightly wilted stalks can be freshened in cold water in minutes. Fresh asparagus can be stir-fried, boiled, steamed or microwaved. Size determines the cooking time, but no matter the size, cooked asparagus should be served tender.

My Mom's Steamed Chicken and Mushrooms

6 dried black mushrooms
¼ cup dried cloud ears (black fungus)
⅓ cup dried lily buds (optional)

Marinade
⅓ cup chicken broth
3 tablespoons dry sherry
2 tablespoons *each* regular and dark soy sauce
2 teaspoons minced garlic
3 slices ginger, slivered
1 teaspoon sesame oil
2 tablespoons cornstarch
½ teaspoon sugar
¼ teaspoon white pepper
✿
¾ pound boneless, skinless chicken, cut into 1-inch pieces
1 Chinese sausage (about 2 ounces), thinly sliced diagonally
4 water chestnuts, sliced

Of all the family-style dishes I had when I was growing up, this is perhaps the dish my mother and many of my relatives would most often serve. It is simple and quick, and while it steams you can work on other dishes.

Serves 3 or 4

1. Soak the mushrooms, cloud ears, and lily buds separately in warm water for 30 minutes; drain. Discard the mushroom stems; thinly slice the caps. Leave the cloud ears whole. Remove the hard ends of the lily buds; tie each bud with an overhand knot in the middle.

2. Combine the marinade ingredients in a large bowl; stir until the cornstarch dissolves. Add the chicken, sausage, water chestnuts, mushrooms, cloud ears, and lily buds; mix well. Spread the mixture in a heatproof glass pie dish.

3. Set the dish on a rack over boiling water in a wok; cover and steam until the chicken is opaque, 15 to 18 minutes.

TIP: For additional flavor and texture, you may add pickled radish strips or Sichuan preserved vegetable to steam along with the chicken and mushrooms.

Singing Mint Chicken

Sauce
½ cup dry white wine
2 tablespoons soy sauce
2 tablespoons fish sauce
2 teaspoons sugar
¼ teaspoon black pepper
2 tablespoons chopped mint

❀

¼ cup cooking oil
6 to 8 fresh mint leaves,
    washed and patted dry
1 jalapeño or serrano chile,
    thinly sliced
2 teaspoons minced garlic
½ teaspoon crushed red
    pepper, or to taste
1 pound boneless, skinless
    chicken, thinly sliced
    crosswise

In this fiery dish, fish sauce, a kitchen essential in Vietnamese and Thai kitchens, is blended with the heat of a jalapeño and the sweet-peppery taste of mint. Just one bite will leave you singing with delight.

Serves 4

1. Combine the sauce ingredients in a small bowl.

2. Heat ¼ cup cooking oil in a small pan until hot but not smoking. Place a mint leaf in the oil and deep-fry until it is glossy, transparent, and emerald green, about 30 seconds. If the oil temperature is too high, the leaf will turn olive green and become bitter. Lift out the leaf and drain it on a paper towel. Repeat with the remaining leaves. Reserve the oil.

3. Heat a wok over high heat until hot. Add 2 tablespoons of the oil, the chile, garlic, and red pepper; stir-fry for 15 seconds. Add the chicken and stir-fry for 2 minutes. Add the sauce and stir-fry until the chicken is opaque, about 2 minutes.

4. Remove to a shallow serving bowl. Garnish with the fried mint leaves around the edges.

Chinese Turkey Vegetable "Lasagna"

Tomato Sauce
1 pound ground turkey or
    lean ground beef
2 teaspoons cornstarch
8 dried black mushrooms

Of all the Italian specialties, I enjoy lasagna the most. But occasionally I find its creamy cheeses and hearty noodles a bit too rich and filling, so I've created a lighter version. Garden-fresh vegetables take the place of the noodles, and tofu and ground turkey maintain the high protein content without adding many calories. A flavorful tomato sauce with a few Chinese seasonings ties it all together.

Serves 8

1. Prepare the sauce: Combine the turkey and cornstarch in a medium bowl. Soak the dried mushrooms in warm

2 tablespoons olive oil
1 medium onion, chopped
2 tablespoons minced garlic
1 tablespoon minced ginger
1½ cups fresh button
    mushrooms, coarsely
    chopped
1 large can (28 ounces)
    tomatoes, drained and
    crushed
1 can (6 ounces) tomato paste
¼ cup mirin (Japanese sweet
    rice wine)
¼ cup soy sauce
2 tablespoons Chinese chili
    sauce
1 tablespoon dried oregano
2 teaspoons sugar
2 teaspoons sesame oil
½ cup (packed) fresh Thai
    basil leaves or regular
    basil leaves, chopped

❀

1 pound firm tofu, drained
1 tablespoon cornstarch
4 medium zucchini, cut
    diagonally into long
    slices ⅛ inch thick
2 Japanese eggplant, cut
    diagonally into long
    slices ⅛ inch thick
Cornstarch for dusting
3 cups (12 ounces) shredded
    mozzarella cheese
¼ cup grated Parmesan
    cheese

water for 30 minutes; drain. Discard the stems and thinly slice the caps.

2. Heat the oil in a wide frying pan over medium-high heat until hot. Add the onion, garlic, and ginger and cook until the onion is soft, about 4 minutes. Increase the heat to high. Add the turkey and cook, stirring, until lightly browned and crumbly, about 3 minutes. Add the fresh and dried mushrooms and cook, stirring, for 1 minute. Add the tomatoes, tomato paste, mirin, soy sauce, chili sauce, oregano, sugar, and sesame oil; mix well. Bring to a boil, reduce the heat, cover, and simmer until reduced and thick, about 30 minutes. Remove from the heat and stir in the basil.

3. Crumble the tofu into a colander and let it stand until well drained. Mix it with 1 tablespoon of cornstarch.

4. In a large pot of boiling water, blanch the zucchini and eggplant until barely tender but not mushy, about 2 minutes. Drain, rinse with cold water, and drain again. Pat the slices dry between paper towels and dust with the cornstarch.

5. Preheat the oven to 350°F. Oil a 9- by 13-inch baking dish and spread a thin layer of sauce on the bottom. Arrange half the zucchini in an even layer over the sauce. Spread a third of the sauce over the zucchini, then sprinkle on a third of the tofu and a third of the mozzarella. Add the eggplant in an even layer, then another third of the sauce, tofu, and cheese. Top with the remaining zucchini, then sauce, tofu, and cheese. Sprinkle the Parmesan on top. (If assembling ahead of time, cover and refrigerate.)

6. Bake uncovered until hot and bubbly, 40 to 45 minutes. Let stand 10 minutes, then cut into squares to serve.

124

Tri-Flavored Chicken

Marinade
2 tablespoons soy sauce
2 tablespoons dry sherry
1 tablespoon cornstarch
¼ teaspoon white pepper

✿

1 pound boneless, skinless
   chicken, cut into 1-inch
   cubes

Sauce
¼ cup chicken broth
3 tablespoons orange juice
3 tablespoons lemon juice
2 tablespoons lime juice
2 tablespoons (packed) light
   brown sugar

✿

2 tablespoons cooking oil
1 teaspoon minced ginger
1 teaspoon *each* slivered
   orange, lemon, and lime
   peel
2 teaspoons cornstarch
   dissolved in 4 teaspoons
   water

Lemon Chicken is perhaps one of the most popular dishes in any Chinese restaurant, and I have created this version for your enjoyment. I think you'll love the fresh fruity flavor of my citrus dish.

Serves 4

1. Combine the marinade ingredients in a medium bowl. Add the chicken, stir to coat, and let stand for 30 minutes. Combine the sauce ingredients in a small bowl and stir to dissolve the sugar.

2. Heat a wok over high heat until hot. Add the oil and ginger and cook for 10 seconds. Add the chicken and orange, lemon, and lime peels and stir-fry for 2 minutes. Add the sauce, reduce the heat to medium-low, and simmer until the chicken is opaque, about 3 minutes. Add the cornstarch solution and cook, stirring, until the sauce boils and the chicken is richly glazed.

In China, the bride and groom are given a pair of chopsticks tied with a red ribbon on their wedding day. It is a symbol that means the couple will stick together for life.

Skewered Hoisin Turkey and Vegetables

Marinade

¼ cup dry sherry or Chinese rice wine

¼ cup soy sauce

3 tablespoons hoisin sauce

2 tablespoons grated ginger

2 tablespoons (packed) brown sugar

1 tablespoon Worcestershire sauce

1 tablespoon sesame oil

2 teaspoons minced garlic

✿

1 turkey thigh (about 1½ pounds), skinned, boned, and cut into 1-inch cubes

16 (10-inch) bamboo skewers

10 fresh button mushrooms

1 *each* green and red bell pepper, seeded and cut into 1-inch squares

1 onion, cut into 1-inch cubes

2 small Asian eggplants, cut into ¾-inch rounds

Here's a delicious treat for the great outdoors—beautiful vegetables alongside sweet and spicy hoisin-flavored turkey, all skewered and grilled to perfection. If you believe in family participation, have everyone build their own skewers. This is outdoor fun for the whole family to enjoy.

Serves 4 to 6

1. Combine the marinade ingredients in a small pan and bring to a boil over medium heat; stir frequently until the brown sugar is dissolved. Reduce the heat and simmer, uncovered, until the marinade is reduced by half. Remove it from the heat and let it cool.

2. Place the turkey in a medium bowl. Add the cooled marinade and stir to coat. Cover and refrigerate for 2 hours. Soak the bamboo skewers in water while the turkey marinates.

3. Lift the turkey from the marinade and thread turkey on half of the skewers; reserve the marinade. Thread the mushrooms, bell peppers, onion, and eggplants on the remaining skewers.

4. Place the skewers on an oiled grill above a solid bed of medium-glowing coals. Cook, turning frequently and basting with the reserved marinade, until the turkey is no longer pink and the vegetables are tender, 18 to 20 minutes. If the vegetables are done before the turkey is cooked, move them to the side of the grill to keep warm.

Home-Style Mongolian "Barbecue"

Meats
½ pound boneless, skinless chicken
½ pound lean pork
½ pound lean beef
½ pound lean lamb

Vegetables
½ pound bean sprouts
½ pound long beans, cut into 2-inch lengths
¼ pound fresh button mushrooms, thinly sliced
2 zucchini, halved lengthwise, thinly sliced
1 large onion, thinly sliced
2 medium carrots, thinly sliced diagonally
1 bunch green onions, thinly sliced

Cooking Sauces and Seasonings
⅓ cup cooking oil
¼ cup minced garlic
¼ cup minced ginger
⅓ cup soy sauce
⅓ cup Shao Hsing wine
⅓ cup sugar
⅓ cup rice vinegar
¼ cup chili oil
⅓ cup sesame oil

If you've ever been to a Mongolian barbecue restaurant, you probably saw the chef cook your meal to order on a huge domed grill. In this home version, you can impress your guests with your skill with a wok. Either way, each diner selects his or her choice of meats and vegetables, places them on a plate, and passes the plate to the chef. You, as chef, ask them how spicy they like it, and proceed to stir-fry and season each portion to order. Try it for a new twist in outdoor entertaining, with a wok set over a portable gas burner. With an electric wok, you can do it indoors or out.

Serves 6 to 8

1. Partially freeze the individual meats for 30 minutes or until firm to facilitate slicing. Holding the knife at a low angle to the cutting surface, cut each meat crosswise into thin 2- by 3-inch slices. Arrange each meat separately on a large platter. Attractively arrange the vegetables in separate groups on another platter. Place the cooking sauces in small bowls or custard cups, arranged attractively and in a logical order near the chef handling the wok.

2. To cook each plate to order: Heat a wok over high heat until hot and add 1 tablespoon of the cooking oil. Add the meat(s) and stir-fry for 1 to 2 minutes. Add garlic and ginger; cook for 10 seconds. Add a portion of the vegetables (add the vegetables that are the hardest or take the longest to cook first); stir-fry until vegetables begin to soften, about 1 to 2 minutes. Add the sauces or seasonings according to each individual's taste. Stir continuously until the vegetables are crisp-tender. Chili and sesame oil should be stirred in last just before removing the food from the wok. Serve with steamed rice.

TIP: Any vegetable may be substituted for the ones above according to what is available during the season. Try broccoli, bell peppers, cauliflower, bok choy, green beans, asparagus, cabbage, napa cabbage, oyster or shiitake mushrooms, snow and sugar snap peas. You might want to blanch the longer-cooking vegetables first to cut down on stir-frying time.

Other possible sauces and seasonings include oyster sauce, hoisin sauce, Chinese chili sauce, crushed red peppers, white pepper, and whole dried chiles.

Penang Pilaf

2 tablespoons cooking oil
4 chicken thighs (about 1½ pounds)
½ cup thinly sliced shallots
¼ pound smoked spicy sausage, sliced diagonally
1 small red bell pepper, seeded and cut into ¾-inch squares
1½ cups uncooked jasmine or other long-grain rice
2 teaspoons minced garlic
½ teaspoon *each* turmeric, ground cumin, and black pepper
2¼ cups chicken broth
1 tablespoon dark or regular soy sauce
1 tablespoon fish sauce
½ cup frozen petite peas, thawed
2 tablespoons chopped cilantro
2 tablespoons chopped fresh Thai basil or regular basil

This easy stove-top rice casserole, named after a city in Malaysia with a large Chinese population, is spiced with my favorite seasonings and loaded with delicious smoked sausage and juicy chicken thighs. Serve as a side dish or enjoy it as a main course with its hearty blend of ingredients.

Serves 4

1. Heat a wide frying pan over medium-high heat until hot. Add the oil and brown the chicken well on all sides, 10 to 12 minutes. Remove the chicken from the pan. Discard all but 2 tablespoons of the pan drippings.

2. Add the shallots and cook for 30 seconds. Stir in the sausage and bell pepper and cook for 1 minute. Add the rice, garlic, turmeric, cumin, and pepper, and cook, stirring, for 2 minutes. Stir in the chicken broth, soy sauce, and fish sauce. Return the chicken to the pan and bring to a boil. Reduce the heat, cover, and simmer until almost all of the liquid is absorbed and the rice is tender, 18 to 20 minutes.

3. Add the peas; cover and cook until heated through, about 2 minutes. Sprinkle with the cilantro and basil.

Baked Black Bean Spareribs

2 medium onions, thinly sliced lengthwise
3 pounds pork spareribs, cut into 2-inch crosswise strips, excess fat removed
¼ cup Shao Hsing rice wine
¼ cup black bean sauce (see Tip, page 82)
6 cloves garlic, crushed
3 tablespoons (packed) brown sugar
1 teaspoon sesame oil
2 green onions, sliced diagonally

This is a great leisure-day dish that can be put in the oven to slowly bake while you watch a baseball game or do your gardening. Leave it to the oven and it will be done when you return, producing a tender, succulent dish of ribs that melt in your mouth. The ribs are blanketed with sweet onions, which gives moisture and sweetness to the ribs. When it is done, serve over steamed rice or pasta.

Serves 4 to 6

1. Preheat the oven to 350°F. Lay a large sheet of heavy foil in a large roasting pan. Sprinkle half of the onions over the middle of the foil and lay the rib strips on top. Add the wine, black bean sauce, remaining onion, garlic, and sugar. Fold the foil over the top of the ribs; fold in the ends to seal the packet. Bake for 1 hour, reduce the heat to 300°F, and continue baking for 1½ hours or until the ribs are tender.

2. To serve, cut the ribs apart between the bones and place them on a serving platter. Pour the pan juices and onions into a pot; remove the fat. Reheat the juices over medium heat and stir in the sesame oil. Pour the sauce over the ribs and garnish with the green onions.

TIP: The pan juices may be thickened as a sauce to glaze the ribs. Transfer the pan juices and onions to a small pan; remove the fat. Add ½ cup chicken broth and bring to a boil. Add 2 teaspoons cornstarch dissolved in 1 tablespoon water and cook, stirring, until the sauce boils and thickens. Stir in the sesame oil. Pour the sauce over the ribs and garnish with the green onions.

Shanghai Red-Cooked Ribs

2 pounds country-style pork
    spareribs or regular pork
    spareribs, cut into 2-inch
    lengths
¼ cup red fermented bean
    curd, mashed
1¼ cups water
⅓ cup dry sherry or Chinese
    rice wine
2 tablespoons regular soy
    sauce
¼ cup dark soy sauce
4 thin slices ginger, lightly
    crushed
3 cloves garlic, peeled and
    lightly crushed
3 green onions, white part
    only
2 small pieces rock sugar *or*
    1½ tablespoons (packed)
    light brown sugar
2 whole star anise
1 tablespoon red rice

This dish was originally created in the Jin Jiang area, near Shanghai. But I first tasted it in California, prepared by my good friend, chef Philip Lo of the renowned Hong Kong Flower Lounge restaurants in the San Francisco Bay Area. I decided to share it with you because believe me, it is marvelous!

Serves 4

1. Trim and discard the excess fat from the ribs. Bring a large pot of water to boil. Add the ribs. When the water returns to a boil, cook for 2 minutes; drain. Place the ribs in a 2-quart clay pot or heavy pan.

2. Combine the bean curd with the water and dry sherry; blend well. Add the remaining ingredients and pour over the ribs. Bring to a boil over medium heat. Reduce the heat to medium-low, cover, and simmer, stirring occasionally, until the meat is very tender and separates easily from the bone, 1¾ to 2 hours. During the last 15 minutes of cooking, leave the lid ajar so the sauce reduces and thickens slightly. Serve over hot steamed rice or noodles.

TIP: A Chinese clay pot (also known as a sand pot or sandy pot) is ideal for making braised dishes. There are many different sizes and shapes available, with glazed or unglazed interiors and exteriors, with loop or knob handles, with or without wire protection. Which to buy is more a question of aesthetics than performance.

Clay pots are fragile, so they need special care. Before using a clay pot for the first time, soak it in water overnight, then drain and dry it before using. Once heated, it can withstand fairly high temperatures, but too rapid a temperature change (like putting a cold pot on a hot burner or a hot pot on a cold surface) will break it. If using an electric stove, you might want to use a heat diffuser on top of the element. The safest way to heat a clay pot is already full of cooking liquid.

131

Stir-Fried Pork with Sweet and Sour Sauce

1 tablespoon *each* dark and
    regular soy sauce
1 teaspoon cornstarch
⅛ teaspoon white pepper
¾ pound boneless pork, cut
    in 1-inch cubes

Sauce
⅓ cup rice vinegar
¼ cup reserved juice from
    pineapple can
¼ cup reserved juice from
    lychee can
2 tablespoons orange
    marmalade
1 tablespoon (packed) light
    brown sugar
½ teaspoon salt
½ teaspoon sesame oil

✿

2 tablespoons cooking oil
½ green and ½ red bell
    pepper, seeded and cut
    into ¾-inch squares
1 teaspoon minced ginger
¾ cup pineapple chunks,
    drained
¾ cup canned seedless
    lychees, drained
¾ cup pitted prunes
2 tablespoons cornstarch
    dissolved in 2
    tablespoons water

My taste buds never grow tired of sweet and tangy flavored dishes. My mom must have made a hundred different versions when I was growing up in the village. I am still always ready for more. Here is number 101, light and simple, and without the deep-frying. Better yet, I use prunes to add color contrast, a sweet tangy taste, and extra nutrients to this all-time favorite.

Serves 4

1. Combine the soy sauces, cornstarch, and pepper in a medium bowl. Add the pork and stir to coat. Let stand for 30 minutes. Combine the sauce ingredients in a medium bowl.

2. Heat a wok over high heat until hot. Add the cooking oil and pork and stir-fry for 2 minutes. Remove the pork. Add the green and red bell peppers and ginger and stir-fry for 1 minute.

3. Reduce the heat to medium. Add the fruits and sauce. Return the pork and cook, stirring continuously, for 2 minutes. Add the cornstarch solution and cook, stirring, until the sauce boils and thickens.

TIP: Because dark soy sauce contains more caramelized sugar than regular soy sauce, you need to continuously stir your mixture to prevent it from burning.

California prunes have no fat or sodium and are high in potassium, vitamin A, and iron. They are not only nutritious, but juicy and delicious as a snack.

Ma Po Tofu

1 tablespoon soy sauce
1 teaspoon cornstarch
½ pound lean ground pork

Sauce

⅓ cup chicken broth
2 tablespoons regular soy
    sauce
1 tablespoon dark soy sauce
2 green onions, thinly sliced

❀

1 tablespoon cooking oil
1 tablespoon *each* minced
    garlic and ginger
2 shallots, chopped
6 whole dried chile peppers
½ teaspoon crushed red
    pepper
1 pound soft or medium
    tofu, drained well and
    cut into ¼-inch cubes
1½ teaspoons cornstarch
    dissolved in 1 tablespoon
    water
2 teaspoons sesame oil

Folk stories tell of an old freckle-faced woman from Sichuan province who accidentally created this timeless masterpiece for her poor family. For centuries, bean curd had been considered poor man's meat. This old woman took the smooth, creamy curd and transformed it from a relatively bland food to what is now known as Ma Po (Chinese for mother and father) Tofu. Adding a bit of marinated meat and spice gave this family something to talk about for generations to come.

Serves 4

1. Combine the soy sauce and cornstarch in a medium bowl. Add the pork, stir to coat, and let stand for 30 minutes. Combine the sauce ingredients in a small bowl.

2. Heat a wok or wide frying pan over high heat until hot. Add the cooking oil and the pork; break the pork into large crumbly pieces with a wok spatula. Stir-fry until lightly browned, about 1 minute. Add the garlic, ginger, shallots, and whole and crushed peppers; cook for 2 minutes. Drain off the excess oil.

3. Drain the tofu again before cooking. Add the tofu and sauce to the wok and cook for 1 minute. Add the cornstarch solution and cook, gently stirring, until the sauce boils and thickens. Stir in the sesame oil just before serving.

TIP: A healthful substitute for ground pork in this recipe would be ground turkey or chicken.

133

Plum-Good Spareribs

Marinade
3 tablespoons plum wine
2 tablespoons regular soy
    sauce
1 tablespoon dark soy sauce
2 teaspoons grated ginger
2 tablespoons cornstarch

❀

1½ pounds pork spareribs,
    fat removed, cut into
    1½-inch pieces
¼ cup plum sauce
1 teaspoon sugar
1 tablespoon chopped
    candied ginger
3 fresh plums, seeded, peeled,
    and cut into thin wedges
½ teaspoon crushed red
    pepper

The Chinese use plums to make an assortment of plum wines and plum sauces. In this dish, I use three forms of plums—fresh, sauce, and wine—to make tangy sweet spareribs. To make this dish even more "plum" delicious, fan-cut several plums for garnish.

Serves 4

1. Combine the marinade ingredients in a medium bowl. Add the spareribs and stir to coat. Refrigerate for 2 hours.

2. Add the plum sauce, sugar, and candied ginger to the ribs; mix well. Spread the ribs evenly over the bottom of a 9-inch heatproof pie dish. Place the plum slices on top and sprinkle with the red pepper.

3. Place the pie dish on a steaming rack in a wok. Cover and steam over boiling water for 20 minutes or until the spareribs are tender.

TIP: The best plums can be found around mid-May through Thanksgiving. To speed up and improve the natural ripening of plums, put them in a loosely closed paper bag. A ripe plum will smell sweet and when placed in the palm of your hand, will give to light pressure.

Asparagus Beef Rolls with Teriyaki Sauce

¾ pound New York steak

While traveling to culinary destinations around the world, I always bring a camera to record any new tasty finds. I discovered this delightful dish at the famous Fook Yuen restaurant in Hong Kong. This recipe was passed on to me by Chef Raymond Lam, one of the best Cantonese chefs in Hong Kong, who is now executive chef at Fook Yuen in San Francisco. These beef rolls can be served as an appetizer or as a main course.

Makes 12 rolls

Marinade

3 tablespoons dry sherry
2 tablespoons soy sauce
2 teaspoons minced ginger
2 teaspoons minced garlic
¼ teaspoon black pepper
2 teaspoons cornstarch
1 egg white

✿

4 dried black mushrooms
¼ pound asparagus tips,
    trimmed to 4 inches
    long
6 green onions (white part
    only)
1 ounce enoki mushrooms *or*
    julienned bamboo shoots
2 tablespoons cooking oil
½ cup Teriyaki Sauce (see
    page 46)
1 teaspoon *each* minced
    ginger and garlic
1 teaspoon cornstarch
    dissolved in 2 teaspoons
    water
Tomato rose

1. Partially freeze the steak for 30 minutes or until firm to facilitate slicing. Thinly slice the steak across the grain into 2- by 3-inch pieces. Combine the marinade ingredients in a medium bowl. Add the steak, stir to coat, and let stand for 30 minutes.

2. Soak the dried mushrooms in warm water for 30 minutes; drain. Discard the stems and thinly slice the caps. If the asparagus stalks are thick (¾ inch or more), slit the stalk down the middle, leaving the upper 1 to 2 inches of the tip intact. Trim the green onions to 3 inches long and split lengthwise.

3. To make each roll, lift a piece of the beef out of the marinade and lay one asparagus stalk across the narrow end. Allow the ends of the asparagus to stick out evenly on both sides. Place half a green onion, a few enoki, and a few slices of black mushroom alongside the asparagus. Roll the beef around the vegetables and secure with wooden picks.

4. Heat the oil in a wide frying pan over medium-high heat until hot. Place the rolls in the pan and cook for 1 minute; do not turn. Add the teriyaki sauce, ginger, and garlic; cover and cook over medium-low heat for 2 minutes.

5. Transfer the rolls to a serving plate. Add the cornstarch solution to the pan and cook, stirring, until the sauce boils and thickens. Pour the sauce over the rolls.

TIP: Any remaining asparagus spears may be used to garnish the plate. Blanch them in boiling water until crisp-tender and arrange attractively in the center of the plate, with the beef rolls around the edges and a tomato rose in the center.

Peppercorn Rib Roast

3- to 4-pound beef rib roast
12 cloves garlic, peeled and
   lightly crushed
½ teaspoon salt
½ teaspoon Chinese five-
   spice
1½ tablespoons toasted
   Sichuan peppercorns,
   coarsely cracked
1½ tablespoons black
   peppercorns, coarsely
   cracked

Ginger Sauce

½ cup mayonnaise
2 tablespoons minced onion
2 tablespoons finely chopped
   green onion
1 tablespoon minced ginger
1 teaspoon sesame oil

Honey-Mustard Sauce

3 tablespoons Chinese
   mustard
4 teaspoons honey

In this country, rib roast is a special-occasion treat, particularly nowadays when so many people are watching their diets. Seasoning the roast with a blend of black pepper and Sichuan peppercorns brings out a pronounced flavor which is ummatched.

Serves 6

1. Preheat the oven to 325°F. Cut deep slits between the bones of the roast and insert the garlic cloves. Combine the salt and five-spice and rub them over the roast. Mix the cracked peppercorns together in a small bowl. Firmly pat them into the fat layer on top of the roast. Place the meat fat side up on a rack in a large foil-lined roasting pan. Roast, uncovered, for 1½ hours, or until done to your liking. Transfer the meat to a cutting board and let it stand for 10 to 15 minutes.

2. Combine the Ginger Sauce ingredients in a small serving bowl; mix well. Combine the Honey-Mustard Sauce ingredients in another small serving bowl; blend until smooth. Place the roast in the center of a large platter. Serve with the sauces on the side.

TIP: A 3-rib roast from the small end of the beef rib is ideal for this dish. This is the end that is adjacent to the short loin, and although it is more expensive than the large end, it has a higher ratio of meat to fat.

Allow 20 to 25 minutes per pound according to the doneness desired. For rare meat, remove the roast from the oven when a meat thermometer reads 130°F; for medium rare, 140°F. The internal temperature will rise another 5 to 10 degrees after the roast is removed from the oven.

Beef and Caramelized Leeks

1 tablespoon soy sauce
2 teaspoons cornstarch
½ pound flank steak, julienned
8 medium leeks (about 1 pound)
4 tablespoons cooking oil
2 tablespoons (packed) brown sugar
3 tablespoons Chinese dark rice vinegar or balsamic vinegar
¼ cup chicken broth
2 teaspoons minced ginger
1 teaspoon minced garlic
6 whole dried chile peppers
1 tablespoon dark soy sauce
1 teaspoon sesame oil

Many of you probably do not realize how popular leeks are in northern Chinese cuisine, simply because you don't see them much in your neighborhood Chinese restaurants. Here, leeks are one of the least appreciated members of the onion family, but they are used in a great number of Peking dishes. In this recipe, leeks stand on their own as a fragrant vegetable rather than just a flavor enhancer. When buying leeks, pick the ones that are no more than one inch in diameter; then you will be assured they will be tender and sweet.

Serves 4 to 6

1. Combine the soy sauce and cornstarch in a medium bowl. Add the beef and stir to coat. Let stand for 30 minutes.

2. Cut the leeks into 3-inch lengths then finely julienne. Heat a wok over high heat until hot. Add half of the oil and the leeks and stir-fry for 1 minute or until the leeks are limp. Add the sugar and 2 tablespoons of the vinegar; continue stirring until the sugar has melted. Reduce the heat to medium-low and add the chicken broth. Continue stirring until almost all the liquid evaporates, about 4 minutes. Remove the leeks and spread them on a serving platter; keep warm.

3. Return the wok to high heat until hot. Add the remaining oil and the ginger, garlic, and chile and cook for 10 seconds. Add the beef and stir-fry until the meat is slightly pink, about 1½ minutes. Add the dark soy sauce, remaining vinegar, and sesame oil; mix well. Arrange the beef over the leeks.

TIP: Julienne cutting of meat means the same as it does for vegetables—cutting into long, thin strips. First slice across the grain, then into pieces of the appropriate length, then cut the slices lengthwise into matchstick-sized pieces.

Genghis Khan Beef

Cooking oil for deep-frying
1 ounce bean thread noodles

Marinade
2 tablespoons soy sauce
2 tablespoons dry sherry
2 teaspoons cornstarch
❀
¾ pound flank steak, thinly sliced

Sauce
⅓ cup chicken broth
2 tablespoons hoisin sauce
1 tablespoon dark soy sauce
1 teaspoon Chinese chile sauce
1 teaspoon sesame oil
❀
2 tablespoons cooking oil
1 tablespoon minced garlic
12 whole dried chile peppers
½ red bell pepper, seeded and thinly sliced
6 green onions, cut into 2-inch lengths
2 teaspoons cornstarch dissolved in 1 tablespoon water

Mounds of snowy white, crisp bean thread noodles make this dish look as if it's floating on a cloud. After one taste of the succulent beef, you'll be on your way to heaven. If you are looking for a familiar and honest down-home dish for the family, this is a feel-good dish with a touch of heat that goes well in any menu.

Serves 4

1. Heat the oil over high heat to 375°F. Add half the bean threads and deep-fry until they puff and expand, about 5 seconds. Turn them over to cook the other side. Lift them out and drain on paper towels. Repeat with the remaining bean threads. Allow the oil to cool; when cool, remove it from the wok and wipe the wok dry with a paper towel.

2. Combine the marinade ingredients in a medium bowl. Add the beef and stir to coat. Let stand for 30 minutes. Combine the sauce ingredients in a small bowl.

3. Heat a wok or wide frying pan over medium-high heat until hot. Add the cooking oil, garlic, and chiles and stir-fry for 30 seconds. Increase the heat to high. Add the beef; stir-fry until barely pink, about 2 minutes. Remove the beef.

4. Add the bell pepper and green onions; stir-fry for 1 minute. Return the beef to the wok and add the sauce. Cook for 1 minute, add the cornstarch solution, and cook, stirring, until the sauce boils and thickens.

5. Transfer to a serving plate. Garnish the edges of the serving plate with the fried bean thread noodles.

TIP: To break bean threads, place the unwrapped bunch in a clean large paper bag or large bowl. With your hands inside the bag or bowl, pull the bunch apart, or cut it with kitchen shears into smaller bunches. The bag or bowl will keep the bean threads from flying all over the place.

To test the proper temperature of the oil, place a small piece of bean thread in the oil. It should puff up immediately. Do not allow bean threads to turn brown; remove them as soon as they puff up. The bean threads may be fried up to 2 days ahead and stored in an airtight plastic bag or container until needed.

Korean Burgers

Patties
1 pound lean ground beef
¼ pound firm tofu, drained, squeezed dry in cheesecloth and crumbled
½ medium onion, chopped
4 green onions, chopped
3 tablespoons ground toasted sesame seeds
3 tablespoons soy sauce
3 tablespoons minced garlic
1 tablespoon coarsely chopped cilantro
2 teaspoons sesame oil
2 teaspoons sugar
½ teaspoon salt
2 teaspoons cornstarch

❀

1 tablespoon cooking oil
6 hamburger buns *or* 4 pita pocket breads, halved
Condiments: Kim chee, cilantro, green onions, hoisin sauce, or your favorite hamburger condiments

Sesame seeds, soy sauce, and lots of garlic infuse these little burgers with classic Korean flavor. Serve them with traditional Korean kim chee (hot pickled cabbage), or use your own favorite burger condiments. East or west—the choice is yours.

Serves 6

1. Combine the patty ingredients in a medium bowl. Mix well.

2. Divide the mixture into 6 equal portions; lightly shape each portion into a patty, ¾ to 1 inch thick. For pita bread, make 8 smaller patties.

3. Heat a wide frying pan over medium-high heat until hot. Brush with the oil. Add the patties and cook to your liking, 3 to 4 minutes on each side for medium rare. Serve in buns or pita bread halves with your favorite condiments.

Smoked Beef Ribs

8 to 10 beef ribs (6 to 8 pounds), kept in one piece
½ teaspoon salt
½ teaspoon black pepper

Smoking Mixture
⅓ cup (packed) brown sugar
2 tablespoons uncooked rice
3 tablespoons tea leaves
2 whole star anise

Barbecue Sauce
⅓ cup hoisin sauce
¼ cup tomato paste or catsup
3 tablespoons oyster sauce
2 tablespoons soy sauce

✿

2 tablespoons chopped green onions or cilantro

In this country, there are restaurants that specialize in barbecued ribs much like those barbecue specialty shops along the streets of Hong Kong. But I'll bet that after visiting all those restaurants, you'll still never have ribs as good as mine. The smoky, rich, caramelized flavor of the tea, rice, and sugar permeate these juicy ribs to perfection.

Serves 4

1. Have the butcher cut the ribs in half crosswise to make the bones 3 to 4 inches long. Trim off any excess fat and sprinkle the ribs with the salt and pepper.

2. Preheat the oven to 500°F. Line a large roasting pan with heavy foil. Place two heatproof steaming trivets or empty water chestnut cans (both ends cut out) on the foil. Distribute the smoking mixture evenly over the foil. Place a baking rack over the trivets or cans. Lay the ribs on the rack.

3. Combine the barbecue sauce ingredients in a small bowl. Brush the ribs on both sides with the sauce, reserving about ¼ cup of the sauce to baste the ribs later. Cover the pan with heavy foil, making a high tent to allow smoke and air to circulate.

4. Bake the ribs for 15 minutes. Reduce the heat to 325°F and continue to bake for 2 hours. Twenty minutes before the ribs are done, fold back the foil and baste the ribs with the reserved sauce. Replace the foil and continue baking for 20 minutes.

5. Remove the ribs from the oven. Cut the ribs apart and transfer them to a serving platter. Garnish with the green onions or cilantro.

TIP: Chinese smoking mixtures can be made of any combination of tea leaves (black, jasmine, or other varieties), brown sugar, and rice. Other ingredients that can be used to give a more complex flavor are bay leaves, five-spice, thin hardwood chips, and tangerine or orange peels.

Spicy Sichuan Lamb

Marinade

1 tablespoon dry sherry
1 tablespoon dark soy sauce
2 teaspoons minced garlic
1 teaspoon chopped fresh
　　mint
½ teaspoon sugar
½ teaspoon ground toasted
　　Sichuan peppercorns
1 teaspoon cornstarch

❀

¾ pound boneless lamb,
　　julienned

Sauce

2 tablespoons rice vinegar
2 tablespoons hoisin sauce
1 tablespoon dark soy sauce
1 teaspoon Chinese chile
　　sauce
1 teaspoon sesame oil

❀

2 tablespoons cooking oil
1 carrot, julienned
2 ribs celery, julienned
2 tablespoons chicken broth
3 green onions, thinly sliced
　　diagonally into 2-inch
　　lengths (optional)

It is typical in Hunan and Sichuan cooking to serve a dish with very little sauce—just enough to coat the meat and vegetables. Those of you who love hot and spicy dishes should enjoy this one. The heat from the chili paste and the numbing sensation from the Sichuan peppercorns balance perfectly in this dish. Carrots add color, texture, fiber, and extra sweetness.

Serves 4 to 6

1. Combine the marinade ingredients in a medium bowl. Add the lamb and stir to coat. Let stand for 30 minutes. Combine the sauce ingredients in a small bowl.

2. Heat a wok over high heat until hot. Add the oil. Add the lamb and stir-fry for 1½ to 2 minutes. Remove the lamb.

3. Add the carrot, celery, chicken broth, sauce, and any juices from the lamb plate. Stir and cook, covered, for 2 minutes. Return the lamb and add the green onions. Stir-fry until the sauce is reduced and glazes the meat and vegetables, about 1 minute.

Braised Lamb Shanks with Vegetables

Braising Sauce

3 cups chicken broth
¾ cup Shao Hsing wine
3 tablespoons sweet chili
    sauce
3 tablespoons hoisin sauce
2 tablespoons soy sauce
1 tablespoon sesame oil
2 whole star anise

✿

2 tablespoons cooking oil
3 pounds lamb shanks, cut
    crosswise into 2-inch
    pieces
6 cloves garlic, peeled and
    lightly crushed
5 slices ginger, lightly
    crushed
6 dried black mushrooms
½ pound whole, peeled baby
    carrots
2 medium thin-skinned
    potatoes *or* 1 pound
    daikon, cut into 1-inch
    chunks
1 medium onion, cut into
    1-inch pieces
3 tablespoons cornstarch
    dissolved in 3
    tablespoons water
2 tablespoons chopped fresh
    mint leaves

Those of you who stay away from lamb because of the strong flavor need not worry with this recipe. The slow-cooked lamb shanks are flavored with a multitude of seasonings which balance the lamb flavor.

Serves 6

1. Combine the braising sauce ingredients in a medium bowl.

2. Heat the oil in a 5-quart pan over medium-high heat until hot. Add the shanks and brown on all sides. Add the garlic and ginger and cook for 10 seconds. Add the braising sauce and bring to a boil. Reduce the heat, cover, and simmer for 1½ hours. Stir once or twice during cooking.

3. Meanwhile, soak the mushrooms in warm water for 30 minutes; drain. Discard the stems and leave the caps whole.

4. After 1½ hours, add the mushrooms, carrots, potatoes or daikon, and onion to the pan. Cover and simmer until the lamb is tender, about 45 minutes.

5. Add the cornstarch solution and cook, stirring, until the sauce boils and thickens. Sprinkle with the mint and serve.

TIPS: Ask the butcher to crack the shank bone before cutting the shank into pieces. This exposes more of the marrow, which enriches the stew.

For convenience and appearance, I use whole peeled baby carrots in this lamb stew. In fact, I prefer to use young carrots in most of my dishes because they are smaller, slimmer, and less fibrous. Baby carrots add a sweet flavor, vibrant color, and extra crunch to any dish. Not only are they great looking, they're great for you, loaded with lots of vitamins and fiber. Best of all, whole peeled baby carrots are available all year.

Fragrant Braised Lamb

Spice Paste

1 cup diced red onion or
   shallots
1 stalk lemongrass, bottom 6
   inches only, minced
2 teaspoons minced garlic
2 teaspoons minced ginger
1 tablespoon (packed) brown
   sugar
½ teaspoon crushed red
   pepper
½ teaspoon cinnamon
⅛ teaspoon ground cloves

❀

2 tablespoons cooking oil
1 pound lean lamb shoulder
   or leg, cut into 1-inch
   chunks
1 can (13½ ounces) coconut
   milk
2 tablespoons dark soy sauce
2 teaspoons minced ginger
½ pound Chinese long
   beans, cut into 1-inch
   lengths
1 red bell pepper, seeded and
   cut into 1- by ½-inch
   lengths
1 small red onion, coarsely
   chopped

Lamb is the preferred choice of meat for millions of people in India, Indonesia, and Malaysia. Here is a very common dish served in all three Asian countries. Cooking lamb in coconut milk and curry results in a rich, flavorful sauce which clings to the meat and vegetables.

Serves 4 to 6

1. Combine the spice paste ingredients in a food processor; process until finely minced, but not pureed. If the paste is too thick, add 1 to 2 tablespoons of the coconut milk to facilitate the processing.

2. Heat a heavy 4-quart pan over medium heat until hot. Add the oil and spice paste and cook, stirring, until fragrant, about 3 minutes. Add the lamb and stir-fry until lightly browned, about 5 minutes. Add the coconut milk, soy sauce, and ginger and bring to a boil. Reduce the heat to low, cover, and simmer for 30 minutes. Uncover and simmer, stirring occasionally, until the lamb is tender, 25 to 30 more minutes.

3. About 8 minutes before the meat is done, add the beans, bell pepper, and onion and cook until the vegetables are crisp-tender. Serve with rice.

146

Noodles
and
Rice

Beef and Asparagus Chow Fun

Marinade
2 tablespoons soy sauce
2 tablespoons dry sherry
2 teaspoons cornstarch

✿

½ pound flank steak, thinly
   sliced

Sauce
2 tablespoons dark soy sauce
1 tablespoon light soy sauce
1 tablespoon salted black
   beans, rinsed, drained,
   and coarsely chopped
1 teaspoon sesame oil
2 green onions, thinly sliced
½ teaspoon sugar

✿

10 dried black mushrooms
¾ pound asparagus, tough
   ends removed, cut
   diagonally into 1½-inch
   lengths
3 tablespoons cooking oil
1 teaspoon minced garlic
1 teaspoon minced ginger
1 pound fresh rice noodles,
   rinsed, separated and
   drained

When in a rush, *chow* some *fun*. You don't even need to boil water for these moist, soft ribbons of fresh rice noodle. Just stir-fry the meat and my favorite vegetable, asparagus, and add the ready-to-eat fun. In no time you are going to have lots of delicious fun!

Serves 4

1. Combine the marinade ingredients in a medium bowl. Add the beef and stir to coat. Let stand for 30 minutes. Combine the sauce ingredients in a small bowl.

2. Soak the mushrooms in warm water for 30 minutes; drain. Discard the stems and thinly slice the caps.

3. Blanch the asparagus in boiling water until crisp-tender, about 2 minutes. Drain, rinse with cold water, and drain again.

4. Heat a wok over high heat until hot. Add 2 tablespoons of the oil. Add the beef and stir-fry until the meat is barely pink, about 2 minutes. Remove the meat from the wok.

5. Heat the remaining tablespoon of oil in the wok. Add the mushrooms, garlic, and ginger and stir-fry for 30 seconds. Add the noodles and stir for 30 seconds. Return the meat and add the sauce. Stir for 1 minute. Add the asparagus and cook for 30 seconds or until heated through.

TIP: Soft, moist fresh rice noodles are sold in many Asian markets. They will keep up to 5 days in the refrigerator, or may be frozen. If they become firm and difficult to separate, place them in a colander and rinse under warm running water. Separate the strands with your fingers and drain well. You may also soften fresh rice noodles in a microwave oven. Place them on a plate and sprinkle with a few drops of water. Cover and microwave for 1 minute. Separate the noodles, cover, and continue to microwave until barely softened, 30 seconds to 1 minute.

For this recipe, dried rice noodles may also be used; cook according to package directions.

Ground Chicken with Bean Thread Noodles

2 packages (1¾ ounces each)
  bean thread noodles
¼ cup dried shrimp
6 dried black mushrooms

Marinade
1 tablespoon soy sauce
1 tablespoon dry sherry
1 teaspoon sesame oil
2 teaspoons cornstarch

✿

2 teaspoons cooking oil
½ pound ground chicken or
  turkey
1½ cups chicken broth
1½ cups julienned fuzzy
  melon or zucchini

The Chinese have a history of giving dishes symbolic names in reference to nature. This traditional home-style dish from northern China, also served in many restaurants, is known as "Ants Climbing a Tree." Scattered bits of ground chicken make up the ants, strings of bean thread noodle make up the tree branches. The delectable combination tastes better than you could imagine.

Serves 4

1. In separate bowls, soak the bean threads, dried shrimp, and mushrooms in warm water for 30 minutes; drain. Discard the mushroom stems and thinly slice the caps.

2. Combine the marinade ingredients in a small bowl. Add the chicken and stir to coat. Let stand for 30 minutes.

3. Heat a wok over high heat. Add the oil and chicken and stir-fry until lightly browned and crumbly, about 1 minute. Add the broth, shrimp, mushrooms, and fuzzy melon. Cover and simmer over low heat for 5 minutes. Add the noodles, cover, and simmer for 5 minutes or until the noodles absorb all the broth.

TIP: Dried shrimp has a distinctive pungent taste which may be a bit too strong for the first-time taster. Cooked baby shrimp may be substituted for the dried shrimp, if desired. Add the cooked shrimp during the last minute of cooking, stirring, only to heat it through.

Seafood Pasta with Thai Pesto

Pesto Sauce

¾ cup (firmly packed) fresh Thai or regular basil
2 tablespoons minced garlic
1 tablespoon grated ginger
1 tablespoon minced cilantro
¼ cup toasted chopped walnuts
2 teaspoons toasted sesame seeds
3 tablespoons walnut oil
1 tablespoon lemon juice
1 teaspoon grated lemon peel
1 teaspoon sesame oil
½ teaspoon salt
¼ teaspoon sugar

❧

¾ cup chicken broth
1 green onion, cut in half
2 slices ginger, crushed
2 slices lemon
8 to 12 small hard-shell clams (10 ounces), well scrubbed
1 pound fresh Chinese egg noodles
2 tablespoons cooking oil
½ pound medium raw shrimp, peeled and deveined
½ pound halibut, skinned, boned, and cut into 1-inch pieces
1 teaspoon cornstarch dissolved in 2 teaspoons water

You might think I am a bit off the wall to have pesto in this book. Look, everybody loves pesto, including me! Here, sweet Thai basil is the predominant flavor, but it is accented with aromatic sesame seeds, cilantro, and quite a bit of spice from the fresh ginger.

Serves 6

1. Prepare the pesto: In a food processor, process the basil, garlic, ginger, cilantro, walnuts, and sesame seeds until finely chopped. Add the remaining ingredients and process until smooth.

2. Combine the chicken broth, green onion, ginger, and lemon in a medium pan and bring to a boil. Reduce the heat and simmer for 5 minutes. Add the clams, cover, and simmer until the shells open, about 4 minutes. Remove the clams. Reserve ½ cup of the broth.

3. Cook the noodles in a large pot of boiling water according to package directions until barely tender to the bite; drain. Place the noodles in a warm serving bowl, add the pesto, and toss to coat evenly.

4. Heat a wok over high heat until hot and add the oil. Add the shrimp and fish and stir-fry until the shrimp turn pink and the fish is opaque, about 3 minutes. Add the reserved ½ cup broth, clams, and cornstarch solution and cook, stirring, until the sauce boils and thickens. Pour the seafood sauce over the noodles and toss.

TIP: To toast walnuts, spread in an even layer in a shallow baking pan. Place in a 350°F oven and toast until the nuts turn golden brown, about 8 minutes. Check the nuts halfway through the toasting time. Gently shake the pan and check for any change in color. Once the color starts to change, toasting will go quickly. Cool and store in an airtight container in the refrigerator for several months or in the freezer for a year.

Stir-Fried Vegetables with Seafood Wontons

Sauce
¾ cup chicken broth
2 tablespoons oyster sauce
1 tablespoon soy sauce
½ teaspoon sesame oil
¼ teaspoon black pepper

Filling
¼ pound medium raw shrimp, peeled, deveined, and finely chopped
¼ pound white fish fillet, finely chopped
½ cup water chestnuts, finely chopped
1 tablespoon *each* chopped green onion and cilantro
½ teaspoon salt

✿

24 wonton wrappers
1 tablespoon cooking oil
2 teaspoons minced shallot
1 can (8 ounces) straw mushrooms, drained
1 can (8 ounces) baby corn, drained, cut in half diagonally
¼ pound snow peas, ends and strings removed
1 small carrot, thinly sliced diagonally
2 teaspoons cornstarch dissolved in 4 teaspoons water

I'm sure you've tried the restaurant favorites of wonton soup and crispy fried wonton. In this recipe, I toss seafood-filled wontons in a hot wok with tender-crisp vegetables. It's a tasty sensation.

Serves 4 to 6

1. Combine the sauce ingredients in a small bowl. Combine the filling ingredients in a medium bowl; mix well.

2. To fill each wonton, place a scant tablespoon of filling in the center of a wonton wrapper; keep the remaining wrappers covered to prevent drying. Brush the edges of the wrapper with water. Fold it in half over the filling to form a triangle; press the edges firmly to seal. Repeat with the remaining wrappers and filling. As you work, place the filled wontons slightly apart on a baking sheet and cover with a dry towel.

3. In a large pot of boiling water, cook the wontons for 2 minutes. Drain, then place them in a bowl of cold water to prevent them from sticking together. Just before you stir-fry, drain the wontons in a colander.

4. Heat a wok over high heat until hot. Add the oil and shallots and stir-fry for 10 seconds. Add the mushrooms, baby corn, snow peas, and carrot; stir-fry for 1 minute. Add the sauce and cook, stirring, for 2 minutes. Add the cornstarch solution and cook, stirring, until the sauce boils and thickens. Add the drained wontons and gently toss to heat through.

TIP: Leftover wonton wrappers can be easily stored in a sealable plastic bag in the freezer for several months. Or cut them into strips, deep-fry and use like croutons as a soup or salad garnish.

Fettuccine with Shrimp and Mushrooms

6 dried black mushrooms

Sauce
¼ cup chicken broth
3 tablespoons mushroom soy
 sauce
1 teaspoon sesame oil
1 teaspoon Chinese chili
 sauce

✿

12 ounces fresh spinach
 fettuccine
2 teaspoons sesame oil
2 tablespoons olive oil
3 tablespoons sliced shallots
2 teaspoons minced ginger
½ pound medium raw
 shrimp, peeled, split
 lengthwise, and deveined
½ small red onion, chopped
¼ pound fresh button
 mushrooms, thinly sliced
1 can (15 ounces) straw
 mushrooms, drained
1 teaspoon cornstarch mixed
 with 2 teaspoons water
2 tablespoons chopped Italian
 parsley

Italian cuisine has many dishes of pasta with mushrooms, but some of them are a bit too rich for my Chinese palate. So, I've lightened this classic combination and given it a Pacific flavor.

Serves 4

1. Soak the dried mushrooms in warm water for 30 minutes; drain. Discard the stems and thinly slice the caps. Combine the sauce ingredients in a small bowl.

2. Cook the noodles in a large pot of boiling water according to package directions until barely tender to the bite; drain. Toss the noodles with sesame oil and place them in a warm serving bowl.

3. While the pasta is cooking, heat a wok over high heat until hot. Add the olive oil, shallots, and ginger and stir-fry for 30 seconds. Add the shrimp and stir-fry until they turn pink, about 1 minute. Remove the shrimp mixture from the pan.

4. Add the onion, dried mushrooms, fresh mushrooms, and straw mushrooms and stir-fry for 30 seconds. Add the sauce, cover, and cook for 3 minutes or until the mushrooms are tender. Return the shrimp to the pan. Add the cornstarch solution and cook, stirring, until the sauce boils and thickens.

5. Pour the sauce over the pasta and toss. Sprinkle parsley over the top.

TIP: When choosing fresh mushrooms, look for smooth, firm, white caps. Remember that size is not a sign of quality or age; choose the right size for the dish—large ones for stuffing, smaller ones for marinating and stir-frying. Store them in their packages until opened, at which time transfer them to a paper bag.

Noodle Pancakes with Pork and Julienne Vegetables

Sauce
½ cup chicken broth
2 tablespoons sweet bean sauce
1 tablespoon soy sauce
1 teaspoon sugar
¼ teaspoon white pepper

❧

4 ounces fresh Chinese thin egg noodles or angel hair pasta
2 tablespoons cooking oil
¼ pound boneless lean pork, julienned
½ cup julienned carrot
½ cup julienned onion
½ cup julienned green onions
¼ cup julienned Sichuan preserved vegetable
1½ teaspoons cornstarch dissolved in 1 tablespoon water

This is one of the best ways to use up all those dibs and dabs of leftover vegetables in your refrigerator. During my poor college days, this is how I cleaned out my refrigerator. It is a tasty way to clean up!

Serves 2

1. Combine the sauce ingredients in a small bowl.

2. Cook the noodles in a pot of boiling water according to package directions until barely tender to the bite; drain.

3. Heat a 6- to 7-inch nonstick frying pan over medium-high heat until hot and add ½ tablespoon of the oil. Place one half of the noodles in the pan. Cook until the noodles are golden brown and crisp, about 2 to 3 minutes on each side. Shake the pan frequently while frying to prevent the pancake from sticking. Transfer the pancake to a plate and keep warm. Make a second pancake using the remaining noodles and oil.

4. Heat a wok over high heat until hot and add the remaining tablespoon of oil. Add the pork and stir-fry for 1 minute. Add the carrot, onion, green onions, and Sichuan pickled vegetable; cook, stirring, for 2 minutes. Add the sauce and cook for 30 seconds. Add the cornstarch solution and cook, stirring, until the sauce boils and thickens.

5. To serve, place a noodle pancake on each individual plate. Pour half of the stir-fried mixture over each serving.

Eggplant Ravioli

1 medium onion
2 heads garlic
Olive oil
1 medium eggplant
1 red bell pepper
1 teaspoon cooking oil
1 teaspoon *each* minced garlic
  and ginger
½ pound lean ground pork
2 tablespoons soy sauce
1 teaspoon Sichuan hot bean
  sauce
1 teaspoon sesame oil
1 tablespoon cornstarch
  dissolved with 1
  tablespoon water

Sauce
¼ cup soy sauce
¼ cup Chinese dark rice
  vinegar or balsamic
  vinegar
1 teaspoon minced ginger
1 teaspoon sugar
1 teaspoon sesame oil

✿

4 green onions
40 potsticker or wonton
  wrappers

Here's a great idea for your next party or family gathering. Shape these delicious pillows, filled with a hearty blend of Italian and Asian ingredients, into half-moons, triangles, or even into the traditional wonton bonnet shape to create a fanciful meal.

Serves 8

1. Preheat the oven to 350°F. Rub the unpeeled onion and unpeeled heads of garlic with a little olive oil. Combine with the eggplant and bell pepper in a shallow-rimmed baking pan and place in the oven to roast. Remove the vegetables as they are done: the bell pepper after 45 minutes, the garlic 1 hour, the onion 1½ hours, and the eggplant 1 hour and 45 minutes.

2. Peel the eggplant and discard the large seed pockets; chop the flesh. Cut off the tops of the garlic heads and squeeze the softened garlic from the skins. Heat the oil in a wide frying pan over medium-high heat. Add the minced raw garlic and ginger and cook for 10 seconds. Add the pork and stir-fry until crumbly, about 1 minute. Stir in the eggplant, roasted garlic, soy sauce, bean sauce, and sesame oil. Add the cornstarch solution and cook, stirring, until the mixture boils and thickens. Let the filling cool, then chill for at least 1 hour.

3. Peel the roasted onion and cut it into julienne strips. Peel and seed the roasted bell pepper and cut it into julienne strips. Combine them with the sauce ingredients in a saucepan and set aside. Cut the green onions into thin diagonal slices.

4. To fill the ravioli, place 1 heaping teaspoon of the filling slightly off center on a wrapper; keep the remaining wrappers covered to prevent drying. Brush the edges of the wrapper lightly with water, fold it in half over the filling to form a half moon or triangle, and press the edges firmly to seal. Place the filled ravioli slightly

apart on a baking sheet and cover them with a damp cloth while filling the remaining wrappers.

5. Bring a large pot of water to a boil over high heat. Add the ravioli and stir to separate. Simmer until the wrappers are tender and the filling is hot, about 1 minute after the ravioli rise to the surface. Meanwhile, bring the sauce to a simmer, stirring to dissolve the sugar.

6. Drain the cooked ravioli and divide them among 8 plates. Drizzle a spoonful of the sauce over each serving and sprinkle with the green onions.

Fried Wild Rice with Mushrooms

2 tablespoons cooking oil
1 teaspoon minced ginger
2 teaspoons minced garlic
2 green onions, chopped
½ cup chopped onion
½ cup diced celery
½ cup frozen peas and
   carrots, thawed
½ cup small cooked shrimp
¼ cup diced cooked ham
4 cups cooked wild rice
Golden egg threads (see Tip)
2 tablespoons oyster sauce
2 tablespoons soy sauce
2 teaspoons sesame oil
Pinch of white pepper
¼ cup chicken broth

On the United States East Coast, most Chinese restaurants prepare a rich, dark-colored fried rice which uses dark soy sauce. This dish gets a similar rich color from California wild rice, which also adds a delightful nutty flavor and chewy texture.

Serves 4 to 6

Heat a wok over medium-high heat until hot. Add the cooking oil, ginger, and garlic and stir-fry for 10 seconds. Add the green onions, onion, celery, peas and carrots, shrimp, and ham and stir-fry for 2 minutes. Reduce the heat to medium-low. Add the wild rice, egg shreds, oyster sauce, soy sauce, sesame oil, white pepper, and chicken broth; toss to mix well.

TIP: To make golden egg threads, heat a small nonstick frying pan over medium heat until hot. Add 2 teaspoons cooking oil and 1 lightly beaten egg; tip the pan to spread the egg thinly over the bottom of the pan. Cook the egg until barely set; turn once and cook the other side, about 30 seconds. Remove and let cool. Cut into thin shreds.

Double Jasmine Rice with Mushrooms

¼ cup jasmine tea leaves
1 cup uncooked jasmine rice
    or other long-grain rice
½ pound fresh button
    mushrooms, sliced
¼ pound fresh shiitake
    mushrooms
¼ pound fresh oyster
    mushrooms
2 tablespoons butter
2 tablespoons finely chopped
    shallots
2 teaspoons minced garlic
2 green onions, thinly sliced
2 teaspoons oyster sauce
Pinch of salt
¼ cup chopped walnuts

This may be the most unusual rice dish I have ever cooked. Cooking jasmine rice in cold jasmine tea imparts a subtle tea scent and jasmine flavor to the rice. The rice is then garnished with sauteed mushrooms, green onions, and walnuts.

Serves 4

1. Bring 2 cups water to a boil in a 2-quart pan. Turn off the heat and add the tea. Cover and steep for 10 minutes. Pour the tea through a strainer and reserve.

2. Return 1½ cups of the tea to the pan and add the rice. Bring to a boil, reduce the heat to medium-high, and cook uncovered until the water is reduced to the level of the rice. Reduce the heat to low, cover, and simmer until the rice is tender, about 15 minutes. Turn off the heat and let stand, covered, for 5 minutes.

3. While the rice is cooking, trim the shiitake mushroom stems and quarter the caps. Cut large oyster mushrooms in half; leave small oyster mushrooms whole.

4. Heat a wok over medium heat until hot. Add the butter, shallots, and garlic and stir-fry for 30 seconds. Add the mushrooms and stir-fry for 1 minute. Add the cooked rice, green onions, oyster sauce, and salt; toss to mix well. Garnish with the walnuts.

TIP: I prefer using small button mushrooms in this dish because they are more eye appealing. However, it does not matter what size of mushroom you choose, as size is not a sign of quality or age. Young mushrooms have their veils attached and have a subtle flavor; open-veiled mushrooms are more mature and more robust in flavor.

Basmati Rice with Nuts and Dried Fruit

1½ cups uncooked basmati rice or other long-grain rice
2 tablespoons cooking oil
1 small onion, thinly sliced
1 tablespoon minced ginger
2 teaspoons minced garlic
2 jalapeño or serrano chiles, minced
½ teaspoon garam masala
½ teaspoon salt
Pinch of white pepper
3 cups chicken broth or water
¼ cup diced dried apricots
¼ cup coarsely chopped toasted walnuts
¼ cup toasted cashew halves
¼ cup chopped pitted prunes
2 tablespoons chopped green onion
2 tablespoons toasted coconut
¼ cup plum sauce

I have become very fond of the spiced basmati rice dishes served in Indian restaurants from London to San Francisco. Here is my version, in which the fragrant rice is topped with toasted nuts, prunes, apricots, and coconut.

Serves 6

1. Soak the rice in water to cover for 30 minutes; drain.

2. Heat a 3-quart pan over medium-high heat until hot. Add the oil and the onion. Cook, stirring, until the onion is lightly browned, about 1 minute. Add the ginger, garlic, chiles, garam masala, salt, and pepper and cook for 10 seconds. Add the rice and cook, stirring, until the mixture is well coated with the oil, about 1 minute.

3. Add the chicken broth and bring to a boil. Cook, uncovered, over medium-high heat until the liquid drops to the level of the rice. Reduce the heat, cover, and simmer until the rice is tender, about 15 minutes.

4. Remove the rice to a serving platter. Sprinkle the apricots, nuts, prunes, green onion, and coconut over the rice. Serve with the plum sauce on the side.

TIP: Garam masala is an aromatic spice mixture typically used in North Indian dishes. It can be purchased in Indian markets and in other well-stocked Asian markets. The mixture typically includes coriander, cumin, cardamom, cloves, cinnamon, nutmeg, mace, and peppercorns. The whole spices are roasted first, then ground to a fine powder in a mortar or spice grinder.

158

Savory Rice in Lotus Leaves

3 cups uncooked glutinous
    rice
3 large dried lotus leaves
½ cup dried chestnuts
8 dried black mushrooms
½ teaspoon salt
¼ teaspoon pepper

Topping

2 teaspoons cooking oil
2 Chinese sausages (about 2
    ounces each), thinly
    sliced diagonally
¼ pound boneless chicken
    thigh meat, diced
4 tablespoons thinly sliced
    green onions
2 teaspoons minced garlic
2 teaspoons minced ginger
¼ pound Chinese barbecued
    pork, thinly sliced
2 tablespoons oyster sauce
1 tablespoon dark soy sauce
2 teaspoons sesame oil
2 salted duck eggs, whites
    discarded, yolks cut in
    half (optional)

You need to allow time for overnight soaking to prepare this festive dish. But once the rice and its treasure of seasonings are wrapped in the lotus leaves, the dish almost takes care of itself. As the package slowly steams, the lotus leaves impart a subtle, smoky flavor and aroma to the savory rice filling. Try this dish and you'll see why it's such a popular dinner party treat.

Serves 6 to 8

1. Soak the rice overnight in water to cover. In another bowl, soak the lotus leaves overnight in water to cover. In a small pan, soak the dried chestnuts overnight in water to cover; drain. Cover with fresh water and parboil for 5 minutes; drain. Soak the mushrooms in warm water to cover for 30 minutes; drain. Discard the stems and cut the caps in quarters.

2. Line a bamboo steaming basket with 2 lotus leaves, allowing the leaves to drape over the sides of the basket; reserve the third leaf. Drain the rice, season it with salt and pepper, and spread it evenly on the bottom of the leaf-lined basket.

3. Heat a wok over medium heat until hot. Add the oil, sausages, and chicken and stir-fry for 1 minute. Add 1 tablespoon of the green onion and the garlic, ginger, and mushrooms and stir-fry for 1 minute. Add the barbecued pork and dried chestnuts and cook for 1 minute. Remove the wok from the heat and stir in the oyster sauce, dark soy sauce, and sesame oil.

4. If using the duck egg yolks, arrange them on the rice. Spread the topping in an even layer over the duck eggs. Sprinkle with 1 more tablespoon of green onion. Place the third lotus leaf on top with the pointed center upward. Tuck the edges of all the leaves into the steamer and place a heatproof plate over the top to hold them in place.

5. Cover the steaming basket and place it over a wok of

rapidly simmering water. Steam over medium heat until the rice is tender and translucent, about 1 hour. Replenish the steaming water with boiling water as necessary.

6. To serve, lift off the plate and unfold the leaves on top of the rice. Remove the top leaf and allow the other leaves to drape over the side of the basket. Sprinkle with the remaining 2 tablespoons of green onion. Serve the rice directly from the basket, placed on a platter.

TIP: Look for salted duck eggs in Asian markets, sometimes covered with a black coating that must be scraped or washed off before cooking. The eggs need to be cooked before using; place them in a pot of cold water, bring to a boil, reduce the heat, and simmer for 10 minutes. Rinse under cold water and shell. Uncooked salted eggs keep for months with or without refrigeration.

 Here's a chopstick tip for travellers in the Far East. Never stick your chopsticks straight down into your rice. This is done only at funerals and in offerings at ancestral shrines. At any other time, it's strictly taboo.

Chicken Fried Rice with Salted Fish

2 tablespoons cooking oil
2 teaspoons minced garlic
1 teaspoon minced ginger
½ pound boneless, skinless chicken, coarsely chopped
2 ounces salted fish, boned, skinned and coarsely chopped (about ¼ cup)
1 egg, beaten
2 green onions, thinly sliced
1 cup shredded iceberg lettuce
2 tablespoons soy sauce
¼ teaspoon white pepper
2 teaspoons sesame oil
4 cups cooked long-grain rice
1 medium tomato, peeled, seeded, and diced
¼ cup chicken broth or water (optional)

Fried rice is everybody's favorite. This particular recipe includes some extra ingredients which make it different from your ordinary fried rice dishes. Crisp lettuce and sweet tomatoes give it a fresh taste, and the pungent taste of salted fish gives it a unique flavor personality.

Serves 6 to 8

1. Heat a wok over high heat until hot and add 1½ tablespoons of the cooking oil. Add the garlic, ginger, chicken, and salted fish and stir-fry for 1½ minutes.

2. Remove the chicken mixture from the wok. Add the remaining ½ tablespoon cooking oil and the egg and lightly scramble for about 1 minute. Add the chicken mixture, green onions, lettuce, soy sauce, white pepper, and sesame oil and stir for 30 seconds. Add the rice and toss for 1 minute. Add the tomato and toss to mix well. Sprinkle in a small amount of chicken broth if the rice is too dry.

TIP: The type of Chinese salted fish packed in oil and sold in glass jars is the most convenient form for this dish. Look for it in Asian markets. Remove as much as you need for the recipe and blot it with paper towels before using. If all you can find is the dried version, soak it until soft before using.

Desserts

Sweet Rice with Mango and Coconut

2 cups glutinous rice
1 can (13½ ounces) coconut
　milk
½ cup (packed) palm sugar
　or brown sugar
¼ teaspoon salt
2 mangoes
2 tablespoons sweetened
　shredded coconut
2 tablespoons chopped nuts

Rice, the main staple of all the cuisines of Southeast Asia, is used in a number of ways—in soups, salads, stir-fries, stuffings, even in desserts. Glutinous (sweet or sticky) rice cooked with coconut milk is a popular base for many tropical fruits, including one of my favorites, rich, creamy mangoes. It's a winning combination.

Serves 6

1. Soak the rice in water to cover for at least 4 hours or overnight; drain. Line a Chinese steaming basket or a colander with a damp piece of cheesecloth. Spread the rice in an even layer over the cheesecloth. Cover and steam over boiling water until the rice is tender and translucent, 20 to 25 minutes.

2. While the rice is cooking, simmer the coconut milk over low heat, stirring constantly, until it is reduced by half (to about ¾ cup). Add the palm sugar and salt and simmer, stirring, until the sugar is dissolved.

3. Transfer the rice into a wide shallow bowl. Pour the coconut milk mixture over the rice and stir gently until evenly mixed. Let stand for 30 minutes for the rice to absorb the flavor of the coconut milk.

4. Just before serving, peel and slice the mangoes. Place a spoonful of rice on each dessert plate and arrange 2 or 3 mango slices alongside. Sprinkle the coconut and nuts over the top.

TIP: Palm sugar is a richly flavored, moist, brown sugar extracted from various palm trees, in a similar manner to tapping maple trees. It is sold in plastic jars in most Asian stores. It will keep for several months in a cool, dry place.

164

Fruity Banana Bundles

Filling
⅓ cup pitted prunes, coarsely chopped
¼ cup toasted shredded coconut
¼ cup finely chopped walnuts
2 tablespoons (packed) brown sugar or palm sugar

✿

3 medium-firm ripe bananas
12 8-inch square lumpia wrappers, thawed if frozen
3 tablespoons flour dissolved in 2 tablespoons water
1 egg yolk beaten with 1 tablespoon water
2 tablespoons *each* white and black sesame seeds
Cooking oil for deep-frying

This recipe is a bundle of sweetness, nuttiness, and good texture. I am almost certain everyone in your family will love it. Best of all, you can make a big bundle in advance, and it will be ready to serve when you are.

Serves 12

1. Combine the filling ingredients in a medium bowl; set aside.

2. Peel the bananas, cut each in half crosswise, and quarter each half lengthwise. For each bundle, place one lumpia wrapper diagonally on a work surface; keep the remaining wrappers covered to prevent drying. Place two banana pieces across one pointed end of the wrapper about 3 inches from the point. Sprinkle with 1 tablespoon of the filling mixture. Fold the bottom corner of the wrapper over the filling to cover, then roll it over once to enclose the filling. Fold over the left and right corners, overlapping them if necessary. Brush the top and sides of the triangle with the flour paste; roll to seal the corner. Repeat to make 11 more bundles.

3. Brush the egg mixture over the top and sides of each bundle. Sprinkle each with white or black sesame seeds or a mixture of both.

4. Heat the oil over medium-high heat to 350°F. Deep-fry the bundles a few at a time until golden brown, about 30 seconds. Lift them out and drain on paper towels.

5. Serve whole or cut in half diagonally. Serve warm or at room temperature.

TIP: Prunes should be used more often for their sweet taste, good texture, and nutritional value. Extremely versatile, they can be used in dishes from appetizers to desserts. Prunes are also one of the tastiest ways to obtain dietary fiber.

Chinese New Year Pinwheels

Dough

1 pound unsalted butter, softened
1 pound cream cheese, softened
4 egg yolks (reserve 2 egg whites)
6 cups all-purpose flour

Filling

2 cups chopped fresh dates
1 cup *each* diced candied winter melon and water chestnuts (Chinese New Year candied fruit)
1 cup diced dried apricots
½ cup minced candied ginger
2 cups chopped walnuts
2 teaspoons Chinese five-spice
2 tablespoons vanilla extract

✿

2 egg whites, lightly beaten
1 tablespoon unsalted butter, cut into small pieces

Sauce

1 cup (packed) brown sugar
1 cup plum wine

Around Chinese New Year in most Chinese communities you will see the streets filled with colorful displays for the celebration—red envelopes, lanterns, and colorful pinwheels blowing in the wind. In the spirit of Chinese New Year, I have used traditional New Year candies as part of the filling for this scrumptious dessert. These unique sweets are available in most Asian markets all year.

Serves 6 to 8

1. Prepare the dough: Cream the butter, cream cheese, and egg yolks together in a mixing bowl. Add the flour and mix to form a smooth dough. Divide the dough into 5 equal pieces. Shape each piece into a flat square; wrap each in wax paper and chill for 30 minutes.

2. Combine the filling ingredients in a medium bowl; mix well. Spray a 9-inch springform pan with nonstick spray. Preheat the oven to 400°F.

3. On a lightly floured board, roll one square of dough into a 6- by 11-inch rectangle about ⅜ inch thick. Brush the top lightly with egg white and spread 1/5 of the filling evenly over the dough, to within ½ inch of all sides. Starting from one short side, roll the dough jelly-roll style around the filling; pinch the ends to seal. Repeat with the remaining dough and filling.

4. Cut each roll in half and arrange the pinwheels cut side up in the pan; space as evenly as possible and brush the edges where they meet with a little egg white to act as glue. Press any exposed pieces of fruit down level with the top of the dough to prevent burning. Dot the pastries with butter.

5. Bake on the middle rack of the oven until the pastry is fully cooked, about 1 hour. If the top is in danger of over-browning before the dough is done, cover loosely with foil. Let cool on a rack for 10 minutes.

6. Combine the brown sugar and wine in a small pan. Bring to a boil, stirring occasionally, until the sugar dissolves. Reduce the heat and simmer until reduced to a heavy syrup that coats the back of a spoon, 5 to 10 minutes. Spoon the warm sauce over the pinwheels.

TIP: Chunks of winter melon preserved with sugar coating (*tong dong gwa* in Cantonese) and similarly candied water chestnuts are available all year in Chinese markets, but they are especially associated with the New Year. They will keep for a long time in an airtight container. If you cannot find these Chinese candied fruits, the recipe will work with other varieties of fresh and dried fruits. Try fresh or dried cranberries, pears, apples, or pineapple. Plump, glossy Medjool dates add a delightful sweetness and chewy texture.

Asian Pear and Lychee Strudel

Filling
½ cup golden raisins
2 tablespoons plum wine
1 large Asian pear
12 canned seedless lychees, drained, cut in half, and patted dry
½ cup chopped toasted walnuts
¼ cup sugar
1 tablespoon finely chopped candied ginger
1 tablespoon lemon juice
Zest of 1 lemon, grated or very finely minced
¾ teaspoon Chinese five-spice powder

✿

When I go to my good friend Chef Klaus Zander's restaurant, the Pine Brook Inn in the San Francisco area, I always order his German strudel. It is delicately sweet with lots of flaky texture. I have taken the liberty of using Asian pear, lychee, and nuts in my version. It is so good that I'm going to ask Chef Zander to put it on his menu.

Serves 6

1. Prepare the filling: Combine the raisins and plum wine in a small bowl. Let stand for 2 hours. Peel, core, and thinly slice the Asian pear. In a large bowl, combine the raisins, wine, pear, and remaining filling ingredients; mix well.

2. Preheat the oven to 375°F. Line a baking pan with foil.

3. Place a towel horizontally on the work surface. Place one sheet of filo horizontally on the towel. Brush the filo lightly with melted butter. Sprinkle with 1 tablespoon of the coconut. Repeat with the remaining filo, brushing

4 sheets filo dough
¼ cup unsalted butter,
    melted
4 tablespoons lightly toasted
    shredded coconut
Powdered sugar for dusting

each sheet lightly with the butter and sprinkling with the coconut. Spoon the pear filling and juices along one long side of the filo, 3 inches from the edge. Fold the edge over the filling. Using the towel to help you lift, roll up the filo jelly-roll style; leave the ends open.

4. Place the strudel in the prepared pan, seam side down. Prick the top surface three or four times with a fork. Brush the top with butter. Bake uncovered until golden brown, 35 to 40 minutes. Let the strudel cool for about 30 minutes. Dust the strudel with the powdered sugar. Using a serrated knife, cut into diagonal slices and serve.

TIPS: Tissue-thin filo dries out quickly when it is exposed to air. After opening the package, sandwich the sheets between two clean dish towels. If the day is very warm, it's good insurance to place one damp towel under the bottom dry towel, and another damp towel over the top dry towel. Keep all the sheets covered except the ones you are working with. Package unused sheets of filo in an airtight sealable plastic bag and refrigerate for up to two weeks or freeze.

Coconut may be toasted in small amounts in a dry frying pan over medium-low heat. Stir or shake constantly until the coconut becomes a light golden brown; remove immediately and cool. Or, toast in the oven like walnuts (see page 150).

Cantaloupe and Papaya with Snow Fungus

½ ounce dried white fungus
  (snow fungus)
4 cups water
4 ounces rock sugar *or* ⅓
  cup sugar
1 cup cantaloupe balls (about
  ½ a medium cantaloupe)
1 cup papaya balls (1
  medium papaya)

Soup for dessert? That's probably the first question that pops into your head when you see this recipe. Dessert soups are common in Chinese cuisine. Cooking this sweet, soothing dessert soup gently in a double boiler or Chinese double steamer jar allows the fragrance of the papaya and the sweetness of the cantaloupe to fuse without boiling and reducing.

Serves 4

1. Soak the white fungus in warm water for 30 minutes; drain. Tear it into large bite-size pieces.

2. In a medium pot, bring the water and sugar to a boil over medium-high heat. Simmer until the sugar dissolves, about 3 minutes.

3. Combine the syrup and white fungus in a Chinese double steaming jar or similar covered container (see Tips). Place a heatproof custard cup or a small rack in the bottom of a large pot and place the jar on top. Cover the jar and add water to the pot to come 2 inches up the sides of the jar. Cover the pot and bring to a boil. Reduce the heat to medium and simmer 45 minutes, replenishing the water as needed. Add the cantaloupe and papaya to the soup, replace both covers, and continue steaming another 45 minutes.

4. To serve, ladle the warm soup into individual bowls.

TIPS: The instructions in the recipe are for a Chinese double steaming jar, the traditional cooking vessel. However, any heatproof covered bowl that will fit inside a larger pot of boiling water will work. Or, you can simply use a Western-style double boiler with a cover.

Rock sugar is the preferred form of sugar for most Chinese desserts. A pale yellow, less refined variety of crystallized sugar, it adds a delicate sweetness and rich flavor and glossiness to a dish. Crush the large crystals before measuring.

Fruit-Filled Yam Pancakes

1 pound yams
1½ cups glutinous rice flour
(sweet rice flour)
3 tablespoons sugar

Prune Filling
7 pitted prunes, chopped *or* 5
dried apricots, chopped
1 tablespoon chopped
walnuts or peanuts
1 tablespoon golden raisins
1 teaspoon toasted sesame
seeds
1 teaspoon toasted coconut

✿

3 tablespoons cooking oil

Yams are hardly used in this country, but when I was growing up my mother used yams in a variety of dishes. This dessert uses yams and glutinous rice flour to make crisp, chewy pancakes filled with an assortment of wonderful sweets. They can be made ahead of time and re-heated at your convenience.

Makes 20

1. Place the yams in a 2-quart pan and barely cover with water; bring to a boil. Reduce the heat, cover, and simmer until the yams are tender when pierced, 30 to 40 minutes. Drain and let cool. Peel the yams; place them in a food processor and process until smooth. Add the rice flour and sugar and process to make a soft dough. Add a little more rice flour if the dough is too soft. (The dough should not be sticky.)

2. Combine the filling ingredients in a small bowl. Place the dough on a lightly floured work surface. Divide the dough in half and roll each half into a 12-inch cylinder. Cut each cylinder into 10 pieces and roll each piece into a ball. Flatten a ball of dough and roll it into a 2-inch circle, making a depression in the center. Spoon 2 teaspoons of the filling into the center of the circle. Gather the edges together over the filling; pinch the edges to seal. Turn the filled ball seam side down. With a rolling pin, flatten it to ½-inch thickness. Repeat with the remaining dough and filling.

3. Heat a little oil in a wide frying pan over medium-low heat. Add as many cakes as will fit in the pan and cook until golden brown, soft, and puffy, about 3 minutes on each side. Drain on paper towels. Repeat with the remaining cakes. Serve hot or warm.

VARIATION: Sweet red bean paste or red date paste (both available in cans in Asian markets) are traditional fillings for this kind of pastry. Try them in place of the prune filling for a more authentic Asian flavor.

Pagoda Fruit Crisps

Cooking oil for deep-frying
12 wonton wrappers

Grand Marnier Sauce
⅓ cup sugar
1 tablespoon lemon juice
¼ cup Grand Marnier
❁
1 cup thinly sliced
    strawberries
1 cup fresh or canned
    loquats, cut in half *or* 1
    mango, thinly sliced
1 cup whipping cream
5 tablespoons powdered
    sugar
¼ teaspoon coconut extract
1 mandarin orange, cut into
    thin segments
¼ cup toasted coconut
4 mint sprigs

When you travel deep into the remote areas of China, Japan, or Korea, you will see many magnificent pagodas. They are architectural wonders which stand straight and tall on sacred grounds. In this recipe my good friend Jan Nix adds delicious fruits in between crispy wonton layers to resemble a grand pagoda. Use your imagination and combine the fruits of your choice.

Serves 4

1. Pour oil to a depth of ½ inch in a 6- to 7-inch frying pan and heat over medium heat until hot. Fry the wonton wrappers one at a time until the wrapper bubbles and just begins to turn golden brown, 15 seconds on each side. Lift out and drain on paper towels.

2. Combine the Grand Marnier sauce ingredients in a small pan and cook over medium heat, stirring once or twice, until the sugar dissolves and the sauce becomes syrupy, about 3 minutes. Let cool.

3. Combine the strawberries and loquats in a bowl. Add the Grand Marnier sauce and stir to coat. In another bowl, whip the cream, 1 tablespoon powdered sugar, and coconut extract until softly set.

4. Place the remaining powdered sugar in a sieve. Shake the sieve over the wonton wrappers to dust them lightly with the powdered sugar. For each serving, place a wrapper on a plate, top with a spoonful of cream and a spoonful of fruit, and repeat for the second and third layers. Arrange the orange segments on top of each crisp and sprinkle with the coconut. Garnish each with a sprig of mint.

TIPS: Other fruits in season, particularly the tropical Asian varieties, may be used in this dessert. Thinly sliced ripe peaches or nectarines are also great choices.

    Don't overcook the wonton wrappers. Remove them as soon as they begin to turn golden brown; they will continue to brown slightly after they are removed from the hot oil.

Ding How Mousse

1 envelope (1 tablespoon)
  unflavored gelatin
¼ cup Grand Marnier
6 ounces white chocolate, cut
  into small pieces
4 eggs, separated
⅓ cup sugar
1 cup whipping cream

Raspberry Sauce
1½ cups fresh raspberries or
  1 package (10 to 12
  ounces) unsweetened
  frozen raspberries,
  thawed
2 tablespoons sugar

❀

2 cups fresh raspberries
⅓ cup minced candied
  ginger
Mint sprigs

Ding how, or "very good," describes this exquisite dessert perfectly. Surrounded by bright red, juicy-sweet raspberries, it is a sinfully rich white chocolate mousse that will leave your satisfied guests repeating the complimentary Chinese expression.

Serves 8

1. Sprinkle the gelatin over the Grand Marnier in a 1-quart pan; let it soften for several minutes. Stir over low heat until the gelatin is dissolved. Melt the white chocolate in the top of a double boiler over barely simmering water. Remove the top pan and set it aside.

2. Beat the egg whites in the large bowl of an electric mixer until stiff but not dry. In another bowl (there is no need to wash the beaters), beat the egg yolks until light and lemon-colored. Add the sugar and beat until the mixture falls from the beater in a thick ribbon.

3. With the mixer on low speed, add the dissolved gelatin slowly to the egg yolks. Add the white chocolate and beat slowly until evenly blended. Fold ⅓ of the egg whites into the white chocolate mixture, then gently fold in the remaining egg whites ⅓ at a time. Whip the cream until stiff. Fold it into the white chocolate mixture until evenly blended. Cover and chill until the mousse is softly set, at least 3 hours.

4. For the raspberry sauce, puree the raspberries and sugar in a food processor or blender. Force the mixture through a fine sieve to remove the seeds.

5. Spoon the mousse into 8 stemmed sherbet glasses or dessert bowls. Top each with the raspberry sauce, fresh raspberries, and candied ginger. Garnish with a sprig of mint.

Steamed Ginger-Flavored Custard

½ cup water
¼ cup (packed) minced fresh
    ginger
⅓ cup sugar
4 egg whites
1 cup low fat milk
1½ tablespoons minced
    candied ginger
4 mint sprigs

This refreshing custard, a very popular dessert in many restaurants in Hong Kong, is light and amazingly delicious—and doesn't use egg yolks. The smooth, velvety texture and touch of ginger taste make it the perfect ending to a light meal. The Chinese believe steamed custards are good for the complexion and increase one's tolerance of cold weather. Not only is it good for you, it tastes great.

Serves 4

1. Combine the water and fresh ginger in a small pan and bring to a boil. Reduce the heat, cover, and simmer for 5 minutes. Strain through a fine sieve and discard the ginger. Let the ginger water cool.

2. Measure one-third cup of the ginger water back into the pan. Add the sugar and cook over medium heat until the sugar dissolves. Remove from the heat and let cool.

3. In a large bowl, whisk the egg whites together with the milk. Whisk in the cooled ginger syrup. Stir in 1 tablespoon of candied ginger. Skim any bubbles from the top of the custard mixture with a spoon. Pour the custard into 4 small custard cups. Cover each tightly with foil.

4. Place a steamer rack in a wok; add water to just below the level of the rack, and bring to a boil. Reduce the heat so the water simmers gently. Set the cups on the rack, cover, and steam until a knife inserted in the center comes out clean, about 20 minutes. Remove the cups from the steamer and let them cool for 1 hour.

5. To serve, sprinkle with the remaining ½ tablespoon of minced candied ginger and garnish with mint sprigs. Serve warm or cold.

Steamed Coconut-Papaya Sponge Cake

1½ cups unsifted cake flour
½ teaspoon baking powder
½ teaspoon salt
6 large eggs, separated
1¼ cups sugar
1¾ cups sweetened shredded
    coconut
1½ teaspoons coconut
    extract
1 teaspoon vanilla extract
2 cups whipping cream
¼ cup powdered sugar
2 papayas
Mint sprig

When I was a young boy, I used to watch my mother make cakes; she always steamed them as most Chinese do. I am still partial to steamed cakes, which can be just as moist and tasty as the oven-baked versions but are lighter in texture and use less sugar, cream, and butter. Try this steamed cake and you'll see why I prefer steamed cakes to baked.

Makes one 9-inch layer cake

1. Grease a 9-inch springform pan; line the bottom with parchment paper.

2. Sift the flour, baking powder, and salt together into a medium bowl. In the small bowl of an electric mixer, beat the egg yolks with ½ cup sugar until light and lemon-colored. Fold in ¼ cup of coconut, 1 teaspoon coconut extract, and the vanilla extract.

3. Using clean beaters, beat the egg whites in the large bowl of the electric mixer until frothy. Gradually add the remaining ¾ cup sugar, beating well after each addition. Continue to beat until glossy peaks form. Sprinkle a quarter of the flour mixture over the egg white mixture. Using a rubber spatula, fold in the flour until just blended, then fold in a quarter of the egg yolk mixture. Repeat, alternating the flour and egg yolk mixtures, blending well after each addition. Pour the batter into the prepared pan and spread it evenly.

4. Place a bamboo steamer in a wok; add water to just below the level of the steamer and bring it to a boil. Carefully set the cake pan in the steamer, making sure it is level. Adjust the heat so the water simmers rapidly, cover the steamer, and steam until a wooden pick inserted in the center of the cake comes out clean, about 30 minutes. Remove the pan from the steamer and let the cake cool on a rack at least 1 hour. Remove the pan sides, invert the cake onto a platter, and peel off the paper.

5. Whip the cream, powdered sugar, and remaining coconut extract until stiff. Halve, seed, and peel the papayas. Cut them lengthwise into ¼-inch slices.

6. Using a long serrated knife, cut the cake into 3 even layers; set the top 2 layers aside. Spread a ½-inch-thick layer of whipped cream over the bottom layer (about 1 cup). Cover it with a single layer of the papaya slices. Place the second layer on top. Repeat with a layer of whipped cream and papaya slices (save 2 slices for garnish). Top with the remaining cake layer. Frost the top and sides of the cake with the remaining cream.

7. Sprinkle a generous layer of coconut on top of the cake. Lightly pat the sides of the cake with a thick coating of coconut. Garnish the top of the cake with the reserved papaya slices and a mint sprig. Refrigerate the cake until ready to serve.

TIP: Some other ripe fruits in season which may be substituted for papaya include strawberries, peeled and sliced peaches or nectarines, and kiwifruit. The fruit should be ripe and soft enough to slice through when cutting the cake. For a variation of this cake, use toasted shredded coconut on the sides of the cake.

When chopsticks arrived in Japan from China around 600 A.D., they were used in religious rituals. Now, of course, they're used for eating, but only in Japan do chopsticks still play a symbolic role in religious ceremonies.

Candied Walnuts

½ pound walnuts or pecans
½ cup sugar
½ cup water
Cooking oil for deep-frying

Adorn your favorite vegetable dish, entree, or dessert with these sweet morsels or just savor them alone as a snack. Whatever your fancy, these crunchy, sugar-glazed nuts are so delicious you won't be able to keep from snacking. Packed in small jars, they make a great gift for friends.

Makes 1¾ cups

1. Blanch the nuts in 1 quart of boiling water for 2 minutes; drain.

2. Combine the sugar and ½ cup water in a heavy 2-quart pan and bring to a boil; cook until clear. Add the nuts and simmer for 8 minutes. Turn off the heat and let stand for 10 minutes. Drain.

3. Heat the oil over medium heat to 300°F. Add the nuts and cook for 5 minutes. Gradually increase the heat to 350°F and cook the nuts until they turn deep brown and glossy and float to the surface of the oil. Stir the nuts often to prevent them from sticking. Using a slotted spoon or wire strainer, remove the nuts from the oil and place them in a single layer on a foil-lined baking sheet, not touching. Let cool.

4. When completely cooled, store the nuts in an airtight container or plastic self-sealing bag in the refrigerator or freezer.

TIP: With the same recipe, try cashews or other nuts.

Ginger Coins

1 cup unsalted butter,
    softened
1 cup sifted powdered sugar
¼ cup minced candied
    ginger
2 teaspoons grated lemon
    peel
2 teaspoons grated fresh
    ginger
2½ cups all-purpose flour
¾ teaspoon ground ginger
¼ teaspoon salt
⅓ cup finely chopped
    walnuts
60 walnut halves

Butter is not used in traditional Chinese pastries, but I prefer its creamy flavor in these gingery cookies. Like other ice-box cookie doughs, this one can be refrigerated for several days or frozen so you can slice and bake the cookies as needed. Serve them as an accompaniment to sherbet or ice cream or enjoy them alone as munchies.

Makes 5 dozen

1. Cream the butter and powdered sugar in a large bowl until light and fluffy. Beat in the candied ginger, lemon peel, and fresh ginger. In a separate bowl, sift together the flour, ground ginger, and salt. Add the creamed mixture, a portion at a time, to the flour mixture, and mix well. Add the chopped nuts and gently mix to combine.

2. Divide the dough in half. Roll each half into a log about 1½ inches in diameter and 15 inches long. Roll each log in waxed paper and twist the ends to seal. Refrigerate the dough overnight or place it in the freezer for 2 hours.

3. Preheat the oven to 400°F. Cut the dough into ¼-inch slices and place the slices 1 inch apart on an ungreased baking sheet. Press a walnut half on top of each cookie. Bake until the cookies are lightly browned, 8 to 10 minutes. Transfer the cookies to wire racks and cool.

Easy Green Tea Ice Cream

1 quart vanilla ice cream
2 tablespoons powdered
    green tea
Few drops *each* green and

A Japanese meal, whether eaten at home or in your favorite restaurant, is never complete without this popular sweet ending. This easy-to-prepare dessert will impress any guest. They'll think you spent hours in the kitchen laboring over this dessert just for them.

Serves 4 to 6

yellow food coloring
Cantaloupe crescents,
lychees, or mandarin
orange segments

1. Let the ice cream stand at room temperature just until slightly softened. Beat until smooth in the large bowl of an electric mixer. Add the powdered tea and beat to mix well. Add one or two drops each of the green and yellow food coloring and beat until the color is evenly blended. (The ice cream should be a pale green.) Spoon the ice cream into a 1-quart container, return it to the freezer, and freeze until firm.

2. Serve the ice cream in individual bowls. Garnish each serving with a cantaloupe crescent, 2 or 3 lychees, or a spoonful of chilled mandarin oranges.

Mango Tapioca Pearls

1 cup small (⅛ inch) pearl
    tapioca
5½ cups water
⅓ cup sweetened condensed
    milk
½ cup coconut milk
¼ cup sugar
¾ cup mango puree (about
    ½ a large mango)
¼ cup diced mango
½ teaspoon coconut extract

Most of us remember eating tapioca when we were kids, but I bet you have never tasted one like this. I combine sweet tapioca pearls with creamy coconut milk and refreshing mango for a cool dessert that is suitable for a light snack any time of day.

Serves 4 to 6

1. Place the tapioca and water in a heavy 3-quart pan. Let stand for 30 minutes.

2. Place the pan over medium-high heat and bring to a boil. Reduce the heat and cook, stirring frequently, until the tapioca is tender to the bite and translucent, about 10 minutes. Add the condensed milk, coconut milk, and sugar. Cook over low heat, stirring constantly, until the sugar is dissolved; do not boil. Remove from the heat and let cool for 30 minutes.

3. Stir in the mango puree, diced mango, and coconut extract. Place in individual serving bowls or in one large serving bowl and chill until ready to serve.

TIP: Tapioca pearls are available in most supermarkets and come in a range of very small to large sizes. I use the smaller ones because they give a smoother texture and more appealing appearance.

Caramel Walnut Popcorn

2 tablespoons cooking oil
½ cup uncooked popcorn
1½ cups walnuts
½ cup butter or margarine
1 cup (packed) brown sugar
¼ cup honey
1 tablespoon grated orange peel
½ teaspoon ground cinnamon
¼ teaspoon Chinese five-spice
½ teaspoon baking soda

Flavored popcorn has become very popular in the last few years. My version, which I enjoy while watching television at home, has just a slight hint of five-spice flavor and added texture from walnuts. You'll need to make a double batch because it won't last too long once everybody gets a chance to try some. No problem, make the popcorn in the wok and you'll be popping corn like there's no tomorrow.

Makes 4 quarts

1. Heat a wok over medium-high heat until hot. Add the oil and popcorn; cover the wok. As soon as you hear popping, shake the wok. Continue to shake until all the popping stops, about 3 minutes. Remove the popped corn to a large bowl. Add the walnuts.

2. Preheat the oven to 250°F. Place the butter in a 3-quart pan over medium heat. Add the sugar, honey, orange peel, cinnamon, and five-spice. Cook until the butter melts and the sugar dissolves. Add the baking soda. Cook, stirring, until well mixed. The mixture will become foamy.

3. Pour the glaze over the popped corn and stir to coat. Spread the mixture in two large foil-lined baking pans. Bake uncovered for 30 minutes, stirring every 10 minutes.

4. Remove the pans from the oven. Immediately transfer the popcorn onto waxed paper and let cool. Store in airtight containers.

Index of Shows

184

Index

188

Metric Conversion Table

Follow this chart to convert the measurements in this book to their approximate metric equivalents. The metric amounts have been rounded; the slight variations in the conversion rate will not significantly change the recipes.

Liquid and Dry Volume	Metric Equivalent
1 teaspoon	5 ml
1 tablespoon (3 teaspoons)	15 ml
¼ cup	60 ml
⅓ cup	80 ml
½ cup	125 ml
1 cup	250 ml

Weight	
1 ounce	28 grams
¼ pound	113 grams
½ pound	225 grams
1 pound	450 grams

Temperature	
°Fahrenheit	°Celsius
155	70
165	75
185	85
200	95
275	135
300	150
325	160
350	175
375	190
400	205
450	230

Linear	
1 inch	2.5 cm

Other Helpful Conversion Factors

Sugar, Rice, Flour	1 teaspoon = 10 grams
	1 cup = 220 grams
Cornstarch, Salt	1 teaspoon = 5 grams
	1 tablespoon = 15 grams